Perfect Phrases for Coaching Employee Performance

Hundreds of Ready-to-Use Phrases for Building Employee Engagement and Creating Star Performers

Laura Poole

New York Chicago San Francisco Lisbon
London Madrid Mexico City Milan New Delhi
San Juan Seoul Singapore Sydney Toronto

2 3 4 5 6 7 8 9 0   QFR/QFR   1 9 8 7 6 5 4

ISBN   978-0-07-180951-1
MHID   0-07-180951-1

e-ISBN 978-0-07-180952-8
e-MHID   0-07-180952-X

Library of Congress Cataloging-in-Publication Data
Poole, Laura.
    Perfect phrases for coaching employee performance : hundreds of ready-to-use phrases for building employee engagement and creating star performers / by Laura Poole.
        pages cm
    ISBN 978-0-07-180951-1 (alk. paper)—ISBN 0-07-180951-1 (alk. paper)
1. Employees—Coaching of. 2. English language—Terms and phrases.
3. Mentoring in business. 4. Performance. I. Title.
    HF5549.5.C8P66 2013
    658.3'124014—dc23
                                                                    2013002320

This is a *CWL Publishing Enterprises Book* produced for McGraw-Hill by CWL Publishing Enterprises, Inc., Madison, Wisconsin, www.cwlpub.com.

McGraw-Hill books are available at special quantity discounts to use as premiums and sales promotions, or for use in corporate training programs. To contact a representative, please e-mail us at bulksales@ mcgraw-hill.com.

Contents

Contents

Contents

Contents

Contents

Preface

Employee performance is a constant concern in groups, teams, companies, and organizations of all kinds. We monitor it, review it, assess it, and strategize around it, always seeking the best we can get out of ourselves and those around us. In these times, when we want (or are forced) to do more with less, managers and everyone in the organization are striving to be more productive, create better results, and get recognition for what we have done. To get more from employees, we offer rewards and incentives, encouragement, motivation—and even punishment when goals are not met or performance slacks off.

Coaching is a relatively new method for achieving professional development. In the business world, coaching has become popular over the past 15 years or so as a method to empower, engage, and develop employees and top talent. Managers are now being asked to be coaches to employees, in addition to being leaders, mentors, supervisors, and trainers. In an organization, one of the key expectations for coaching is to improve employee performance.

To do that in a sustainable, positive way, coaching techniques can help employees tap into their own knowledge, skills, and motivation, to become more efficient and effective contributors.

The very act of coaching inspires engagement from employees because you are seeking their true thoughts, opinions, skills, and abilities and allowing these to come to the forefront. With judicious and appropriate use of coaching, employees can start "firing on all cylinders," taking ownership and pride in their work.

Thus, this book was written to help you learn some coaching techniques, questions, and phrases to use with your employees to improve performance across the board—including your own.

This book is written for managers at nearly all levels of an organization, as well as entrepreneurs and community leaders. I assume that you, the reader, have some sort of leadership position in which you seek to improve the performance of employees you manage directly. You might find that these techniques work in other areas of your life, as well, such as during a charity fundraiser or when serving in professional association committees.

Overview of the Book

I begin with an introduction that outlines what coaching is, when to use it (and when not), how solution-focused coaching works, and other tools for getting the most out of this book. I recommend that you carefully read this introduction, as it sets the stage for optimal use of what follows. Refer back to it frequently. This rest of the book is divided into four major sections.

Part One is all about coaching new hires. Bringing a new employee up to speed presents a unique set of coaching challenges. Not only are you learning about your new team member, he or she is learning everything about the company and procedures, from square one. I offer some key questions and phrases you can use to guide their journeys as they come on board.

Part Two is about coaching existing employees, from general tips to finding coachable moments (such as performance review), goal-setting techniques, problem solving, change initiatives, and a crisis. I then discuss how to coach low, average, and top performers.

Part Three explores the unique aspects of coaching teams. This section covers everything from starting up and chartering teams to brainstorming, processes, performing, check-in, and project completion.

Part Four covers how to use coaching techniques with those who are higher in the chain of command. Note that you probably won't do direct coaching for your superiors, but you can certainly use some coaching-style questions and techniques to elicit the bigger picture, mission, vision, and goals. In turn, you can use this information to improve your own performance and communicate with those around you to keep everyone on the same page.

Acknowledgments

I give my heartfelt thanks to Nicoa Dunne for her thoughtful, constructive guidance on the outline and overall content. Thanks also to John Woods of CWL Publishing for trusting me with this book. Thanks to my most excellent husband, Eric, for listening to me as I got excited about the project and cheering me on as I wrote it. And to our daughter, Joanna, for being the heart inside the work.

Introduction
Coaching: What It Is and Is Not

What is *coaching*, exactly? If you've ever played any kind of sport (team or individual), you've had a coach. This was someone who taught you skills, organized the team or class, and helped you do your very best each time you played. In the realm of professional sports, athletes may have a specialized coach just for one tiny aspect of their game. For instance, some golfers hire putting coaches, and some basketball players have coaches just to help them improve free throws.

Outside of the sports arena, "coaching" has a broader meaning but still carries the power and lifetime impact that traditional coaching brings to a person's experience. According to the International Coach Federation, *coaching* is "partnering with clients in a thought-provoking and creative process that inspires them to maximize their personal and professional potential." Coaching has been growing in popularity over the past decade or two as a way to grow professionally and personally and achieve one's goals. Executives are recognizing the value of coaching and taking advantage of it for themselves and their organizations. Managers and leaders are frequently expected to add coaching skills to their repertoire of tools to use in the workplace. Thus, this book focuses on how to *coach* employees so they can perform at their highest potential.

Some common areas in which employees may benefit from and, in many cases, crave coaching include the following:

- Growing into a new role and applying new skills;
- Dealing with multiple responsibilities, projects, timelines, and budgets (time and task management);
- Advancing in one's career path;
- Balancing work and life (or, for some, separating work and life);
- Improving interpersonal and communication skills;
- Launching a pet project and seeing it through to completion;
- Facing interpersonal issues with others in a team environment.

Coaching is *not* mentoring, advice giving, training, counseling, or therapy (although it may seem to overlap some of these methods). Coaching assumes individuals know what they want and need, and the process helps them uncover it, take ownership of it, and move forward in a productive, sustainable way. Coaches help people unlock their inner genius, find a sustainable path to change, and hold them accountable for their action items and commitments. It always focuses on what the clients *want* (not what they don't want) and how to get it. Coaches help clients focus on the future, looking to the past to learn lessons for moving forward, not to point fingers of blame. Thus, coaching isn't very effective when people simply want to complain about something or place blame for a problem somewhere.

With that in mind, here is a short list of situations in which coaching is *not* appropriate and may require you to exercise your authority or give a referral to other resources (such as an employee assistance program):

- Untreated mental illness or physical health problems (depression, chronic disease) that require a doctor's evaluation;
- Serious personal or family problems (divorce, money issues) that are best referred to a professional counselor or therapist;
- Major legal, ethical, or policy violations (embezzlement, harassment) that require punitive action;
- Any emergency state of crisis (physical damage to the office, layoffs) when people might be simply in "survival" mode.

Being clear on when to coach and when *not* to coach will make your life easier and ensure you don't venture into a conversation that is better left for a professional. When in doubt, ask for guidance from your human resources partner or professional services resources supporting your organization.

General Principles

Before we begin with specific phrases to use, it would be helpful for you to learn about some basic concepts that inform the process of coaching. These are the core concepts and keys to good coaching. A professional coach takes the following approaches:

- The client (person receiving coaching) is powerful and resourceful (not "broken" or "wrong").
- The coaching is focused on getting a result in the future (not on dwelling in the past).

- The client must focus on something that is within his or her control to change.
- The actions identified are cocreated by the coach and client.
- The coach asks powerful questions that help the client discover new opportunities and their own personal inner resources.
- The client identifies how he or she will hold him- or herself accountable.
- The coach holds the client accountable for action steps and commitments.

You can certainly use these principles in your workplace when coaching employees. Remember to respect and validate your colleagues' opinions and ideas, help them focus on how to get what they want, and ask questions that bring their own unique genius to the forefront.

Coaching Process

Solution-focused coaching tends to follow a very basic format, from which you can vary as needed. There are four primary questions to be asked:

- What do you really want?
- Why is it important to you?
- How will you get it?
- How will you stay committed and hold yourself accountable?

These questions seem deceptively simple. They can lead to great breakthroughs if you know what each one means and how you're soliciting responses.

Asking "What do you really want?" is a step that should not be skipped. Never assume that you know what an employee wants. You might think someone is coming to you for a particular reason, but they have a very different issue in mind—or, an entirely different take on the issue you imagined. Respecting their opinions and viewpoints by asking these questions ensures a number of things. First, you aren't making any assumptions or creating the agenda for someone. Second, you validate and acknowledge their thoughts and help them feel truly heard, a valuable technique for building rapport and engagement. Finally, by letting go of your own assumptions and listening to someone else, you open yourself to learning more about your employee and possibly even your company.

When asking "What do you want?," you are seeking an answer that is very specific and positive. "I *don't* want . . ." is not something for which you can coach! Also, the desire should be specific and measurable (see Chapter 6, Goal Setting) so that the result becomes obvious when it's been achieved.

"Why is it important to you?" may seem like an obvious question, but the response is not always so apparent. When asking this of an employee, encourage him or her to go beyond immediate reasons like "because I should" or "because I want to" or even "I want to get promoted." You can connect their immediate wants with their personal values and goals, as well as the department, group, or company mission. This can be incredibly motivating to someone! Some great follow-up questions include:

- What would it *do* for you?
- Who else would be affected?
- How does achieving this help you live your values?
- What is it costing you not to have this?
- What are you afraid will happen if you *don't* get what you want?

"How will you get it?" is the key action question. By asking this and leaving space for a thoughtful answer, you help the employee come up with a plan of action. There may be some brainstorming at first, which is fine; then you can help him or her sort through the options. The employee may need you, as a manager or leader, to provide information about other tools and resources available. To empower someone to take ownership of reaching a particular goal, be sure to keep the focus of the conversation on what that person can do. Some associated questions you can ask are:

- How well is what you are currently doing getting you what you really want?
- How can you get this with less cost?

The final question, "How will you stay committed and accountable?" is a good way to build in accountability. It's also a good time for contingency planning in case something goes wrong. Invite the individuals to tell you how they will commit and stay on track, and help them hold themselves accountable for their actions.

Consider the following real-world example of how a solution-focused coaching session might go in the workplace.

Sandy, a manager in the business-to-business (B2B) sales division of a multinational company, is approached by one of her salespeople, Dennis. He has worked for the company for about four years, and his revenue numbers are not the lowest, but neither are they the highest. He's about the middle of the pack. Dennis asks to see Sandy briefly in her office for a private conversation.

"Sandy, I'd like to talk to you about the possibility of my getting a raise. I know the economy has been off, which is affecting everyone's sales numbers, but I am a solid producer and I've been here long enough to get more than a cost-of-living bump."

She responds, "Okay, Dennis, let's talk about that a little bit. How large a raise did you have in mind?"

He replies, "I was hoping for a 20 percent raise."

"That's a pretty big increase. I can let the executive vice president (EVP) know your request, if you want. I'm going to recommend you do all that you can to position yourself for success. Do you mind if I coach you around this?"

"Yes, absolutely, that would be great!"

Note that Sandy has asked permission to coach Dennis. He is free to opt out, and she won't jump in without his approval. Coaching works best when the recipient knows what is coming and can respond appropriately. At this point, Sandy knows specifically what Dennis wants: a 20 percent pay increase. He has recognized the value of Sandy coaching him—to do whatever is in his control to get the outcome he wants—and readily agrees.

"Okay, so let's say you get a 20 percent raise. What will that do for you?"

"Well, here at work I'll feel valued and committed. I like recognition for my hard work, and I would feel validated about what I've put into this job. It would also motivate me to keep doing well."

Sandy responds, "You are definitely appreciated, and I want you to feel good about what you do for us. What would it mean to you to feel validated?"

He thinks a moment and says, "I really want to feel like my work makes a difference here—and not just in the bottom line. I believe in this company, that's why I have stuck around. I want to know that this company believes in *me* as well. I guess I want proof of that. It will give me a sense of security."

"I can see that your sense of contribution and value are big motivators for you. Let me ask this: What about the extra money? What would *that* do for you?"

"Oh gosh, Barb and I have plans to make some house repairs; plus, we want to be able to put more into D.J.'s college fund. And maybe we could finally take that dream trip to Ireland we've been talking about for so long!"

"Wow, that sounds great!"

Dennis has opened up about what this raise would signal to him, and Sandy is able to pick out some of his values: recognition, validation, security, and commitment. It's also fairly clear that his family is important to him, and the extra money would allow him to create the future they've dreamt about. Sandy starts asking questions to help Dennis lay out a plan for how he can position himself for a raise.

"So, Dennis, what are *you* going to do to position yourself so that you are considered for this raise?"

"Well, I've been working hard on getting my sales numbers up. I've brought in a few new clients, and when the contracts are signed, that will solidly impact my numbers. Plus, I have been working on renewing contracts with some existing customers, which will mean a lot of repeat business for us."

"That's great to hear and very promising! What else might you do to prove your value to the EVP?"

"Well, I really enjoyed working with our intern last summer. I seemed to have a knack for teaching her stuff. I thought I'd put together some training materials so that all our interns and even our new salespeople and existing team can share the knowledge."

"That's an innovative idea that would really have some value! Tell me a bit more about it."

In the space of a few questions, Sandy has invited Dennis to outline what he's currently doing and some ideas for how he can demonstrate his value. His creativity is coming forth—his idea for training was unexpected, but she immediately sees the value in it. They brainstorm for a while on that project.

Sandy then asks, "What else comes to mind for improving your chances for that raise?"

"Well, I confess, I've had issues with keeping my travel expenses reasonable in the past. I'm going to work hard at minimizing them this year, and I think I can do a lot better. Now that we have sophisticated video conferencing, I don't need to travel as much, but I do need some help learning the technology, so I am going to work on that."

"That's very insightful of you. You may not know this, but our video-conferencing vendor often has training sessions at its office nearby; and if you want, I can see about getting you into the next one."

Dennis has voiced his awareness of his areas of weakness and already has some ideas for improvement. Sandy offered to connect him with some resources he might not have been aware of (he gratefully accepted). After they talk about a few more of his ideas, she asks a few more pointed questions.

"All right Dennis, I see that you are taking control of what you can to make sure you are worth the raise! How will you make sure we all *know* about what you've done? Raises may be available before the next performance review, so how will you toot your own horn?"

"Good question! Hmm, let me think. [He ponders.] I'd like to keep track of my accomplishments and positive changes. Maybe I could write it all up into a proposal or justification to send to the EVP. Come to think of it, I should probably meet with him a few times along the way to start mentioning some of what I'm doing and what I'm aiming for."

"Sounds like a plan to me! How can I help you along the way?"

"Would you mind looking at my rough draft once or twice? That would be helpful. Any tips you can pass along for talking to the EVP would also be good."

"Sure, I'd be happy to take a quick review of your document. I'll also check in with you about some of those tasks you've set out to do. You can get on our EVP's calendar at your discretion, and I'm happy to talk to you about how best to present yourself."

"Sandy, thank you! I was nervous coming to talk to you about this, but I feel calmer now, even excited to get going!"

"That's great! Keep up that momentum, and I'll do all I can to support you!"

Sandy has helped Dennis come up with a plan and will help him hold himself accountable by checking in on him. As a good manager, she is supporting him with resources that he might need (such as the training class). Notice that at no point did she promise he would get a raise; she kept Dennis focused on his own tasks and goals so he could put his energies into things within his control.

Manager as Coach

We recognize that as a leader in your organization, you probably have to fill a lot of different roles from time to time—mentor, advisor, trainer, manager, and now coach. Professional coaches, who don't have to manage, would not be involved in telling a client what to do or how to do it; they would focus only on helping the client, through conversations and powerful questioning, to create change in areas under their control. Coaching is about helping someone take responsibility in all areas of their experience at work, at home, with others, with themselves.

However, as a manager, you need to wear a lot of other hats at the same time. You are in the trenches, right in the context of the working world, and your knowledge of the company, industry, and executives is useful to your employees. The coaching phrases and questions you find here will overlap with your other roles and techniques to a certain extent. These examples are based on real-world approaches to the situations and phrases presented in this book.

More employees are beginning to seek (and expect) coaching as part of their development and career path. With this trend, it is expected that more and more employees are ready to receive coaching from you, their manager. Someone has to be ready for change and ready to work to get the most out of being coached and committing to this two-way partnership. With some luck, you've got (at least a few) motivated, smart, engaged employees ready to roll their sleeves up and get to work; for those who aren't, coaching skills can be just what you need to get their attention. You can use coaching techniques to inspire all employees to greater heights. In some cases, they won't even know what happened—they'll just know they feel better, are moving forward toward their goals, and feel more engaged.

In addition, don't forget to learn to coach yourself with these skills. Aspiring to be coachable yourself will allow you to be a better coach to your team. Always be open to what you can learn from everyone around you—from those you manage to those in the upper echelons of the executive suite. Your own skills and knowledge will grow if you keep a curious mind and ask the right questions of yourself and others.

Who Do I Coach and When Do I Coach Them?

In the workplace, you are probably expected to coach those you manage, or those who require your leadership and influence. This is typical. You probably won't be asked to coach someone roughly equal to you, although they might come to you for advice or ideas, in which case you could use some of the coaching-style questions you find in this book, if appropriate. You almost certainly won't be asked to coach someone above you. (However, see Part Four, Perfect Phrases for Using Coaching Techniques with Superiors, which is about phrases and questions to use with upper leadership, which of course you can also incorporate into your approach with other employees.)

With teams, you can use coaching techniques most effectively if you are the clear or official team leader; you may find ways to incorporate some techniques even when you are a team member and not a leader. It is all about creating buy-in and influencing others to help themselves, which in turn helps the team and your personal success associated with your organization. If you serve in community or professional organizations, like a homeowner's association or a chapter of an industry professional group, you can take advantage of your role to use some phrases to help move the group toward getting things done— toward achieving goals and ultimate success with greater ease and enthusiasm.

The opportunities for coaching may be planned or might crop up unexpectedly. This book specifically covers coachable moments such as annual reviews, onboarding of new hires, and times of change. A simple "Hey, can I talk to you for a minute?" can lead to an excellent opportunity for impromptu one-on-one coaching.

Questions (and Answers)

One thing you may have already noticed about the phrases above and in the rest of this book: many of them are *questions*. The process of coaching involves asking powerful questions, which bring forth the client's (employee's) personal resources to create a good outcome. To be effective as a coach, make sure you don't rattle off a question in haste and forget to carefully listen to the response. From a response, you can get the most important information to fuel your next questions and help you most effectively coach the person. It helps to be genuinely and authentically curious. Give your attention to your employee, let her see how you are engaged with her in that moment. Make this conversation all about *her*.

The other side of asking questions, of course, is *listening to the response.* If you are engaging in the moment, then you are mindful of creating a space that gives your employee time to come up with a response. Listening intently and creating a positive, safe space for a two-way dialogue will result in sustainable ownership for moving forward on the opportunity or challenge the employee is facing. By asking and then listening (and then discussing), you create true engagement in the workplace. Employees will feel that their voices, opinions, and thoughts are truly heard and valued, and they will feel empowered to take action toward their goals.

To make the most of any kind of coaching opportunity, keep in mind the following tips:

- Respect confidentiality if the employee comes to you with a private or sensitive matter.
- Foster an atmosphere of trust and safety for employees to bring issues to you.
- Respect each employee's point of view (you don't have to agree with it, just respect it).
- Stay focused on the positive—what you and the employee want to happen.
- Avoid placing blame or letting the employee complain rather than seeking a solution.

After you have had a coaching session, back up all your words with actions and help your employee do the same. What did *you* agree to do? What did *they* agree to? What commitments did you make to your employee, and what did he or she make to you? Keep everyone on task, and check in as needed to see how things are going.

Part One

There is a steep learning curve for anyone starting a new job. Even if the employee is experienced in your industry or type of work, he or she will be learning your group's unique culture, procedures, techniques, systems, office layout, colleagues' work styles, leadership, and more. That's a lot to take in! Someone recently promoted has to learn new job roles and responsibilities, which can be challenging. A transferred employee might have to learn all new job skills as well as the culture in his or her new department. A new employee usually wants to be productive as fast as possible and needs your support, guidance, and coaching to get there. This section offers phrases and techniques for supporting employees in new positions—newly hired, recently promoted, or transferred workers—as they get up to speed.

Remember, set your new employees up for success by offering more than just coaching: engagement, appropriate training, responsiveness, tools, and resources.

Chapter 1
Encouraging Engagement

E*mployee engagement* is a hot phrase in the business and management world. An engaged employee is one who is excited and visibly involved in the work of the organization, beyond just putting in enough hours to get a paycheck. When workers are engaged, they commit to and seek to further the company's mission. Engaged workers are far more productive; research has found that companies with highly engaged employees more than doubled revenues compared with less engaged companies.

Creating an atmosphere for highly engaged employees is heavily influenced by their experiences when they are first hired. New employees are frequently excited about their new opportunities, and you can leverage this excitement to foster true engagement by aligning what matters most to the organization with what matters to the employees. Ideally, they know about the companys' missions or visions from their own research and hiring interviews. Once they are officially on board, you have an opportunity to make it truly personal and cement engagement right from the start.

Connecting to the Big Picture

It's a new employee's very first day in your department. She arrives on time and is sitting comfortably in your office, ready for her orientation. You start with a little chitchat to set her at ease, then you get down to business. You begin by explaining some of the bigger picture of the company as a whole, eventually getting to how the new employee will be contributing.

- At this company, our mission is [state mission] .... That is our purpose for being here!
- To do that, we [state what you produce or provide] ....
- In this department, we contribute by [clarify what your team does] ....
- Our tasks are mission-critical because ... [identify what we do, how it impacts clients and customers, and why it matters].
- In your role here, you will be [state purpose of this job position, expectations] ....
- Being productive and successful in your role enables you to be rewarded and recognized [list potential rewards].
- We also hope you'll feel personal satisfaction in how you contribute to our mission.

For a conversational example, imagine that you are a manager in an insurance company. You are describing these big-picture concepts to your newest team member. You say, Here at Big Life, our mission is to create and enhance our customers' financial security. We do this by providing a variety of life insurance, investment, and planning resources. The Communications Department is responsible for making sure our customers understand our printed and online materials, so we help educate the public on what we offer. In your job as our new Web editor, you will be helping us maintain a high quality of online materials so that we can help those who need us. Successfully doing so positions you nicely for bonuses, raises, and promotions, and can be very satisfying knowing you've made a difference for our customers and the team."

In just a few sentences, you have connected a single person's effort to the broader mission of the company—something that can be highly motivating, especially for a worker coming in at an entry-level position.

You can then follow up by adding more pertinent information.

- Our core values are [list values] …
- We pride ourselves on …
- We commit to …
- We encourage and reward [certain behaviors] …
- We value our employees, and we're excited to have you on board.

Encouraging Personal Connection

This is a critical step in creating an environment for strong employee engagement right from the beginning. It's not enough to just deliver the corporate message to people and hope they receive it. You need to help them actively connect it to their own goals and values. You can get more personal and ask some open-ended questions. Some of these will sound like interviewing questions (and they might well have been used in the hiring process), but they serve an important purpose here. The idea is to elicit worker commitment and engagement by letting them voice what matters most to them in their own words.

- What attracted you about our company when you applied for this position?
- What appeals to you about working for this company?
- What are you excited about?
- How do you see yourself contributing to our mission? Why is that important to you and your career goals?

A critical step here is to acknowledge that you have truly heard what the person has shared with you. You need to "replay" it back, perhaps paraphrasing a bit, to show him that you listened. This often-skipped step validates the new employee's beliefs and values and makes them feel respected.

- I can see how your professional goals [be specific] fit in with our mission! I see it as a good match, and I hope you do, too.
- We're excited to have you here, and I look forward to working with you as you grow in this role and this company.

Setting Expectations

A large part of coaching (and managing) is direct, honest communication. Be very clear with your new employees about what is expected of them. They need to know up front (and probably be reminded) about the company's goals for their jobs and performances.

- You will have an onboarding period [length of time]. During that time, you will be trained and brought up to speed.

- At the end of your training, we expect you to be able to . . . .

- At the end of your onboarding period, we expect . . . .

- We will have a meeting at the end of your training to discuss how it went, where you are, and what's next.

- We know you will be learning a whole lot in a short time. We don't expect you to be perfect right away.

- We have various training materials for you [a video, tutorials, written manuals, peer demonstrations, workshops, etc.].

Chapter 2
Learning about Them

To work with someone effectively—especially to coach their performance—you need to know about that person. What makes him tick? How does she work most effectively? How does your team like to be managed? What are their goals and strengths, and how can you leverage that information to help them improve and grow? (If you were directly involved in the hiring process and interviewed people before making the hiring decision, you might already know some of the answers to the questions I present here.)

Learning Your Employees' Goals

Knowing an individual employee's personal and professional goals is a valuable tool when managing him. If you know what someone hopes to accomplish, you can help him make the connection between work tasks and personal achievements. When you can connect them with the means and resources to meet his goals, he can become not only engaged but excited, committed, and loyal.

- What are you passionate about? Or, What matters most to you?
- What are your long-term career goals? What are your personal goals?
- What do you want to achieve in this position?
- What skills do you want to pick up or improve on?
- What do you want to learn?
- Beyond learning the ropes and getting up to speed, what are some of your short-term goals?
- How can I support you in achieving your goals?

Be sure to take notes about the person's responses; you might well revisit these questions and ask him again at performance reviews and other check-ins.

Determining Employee Strengths

We all have our strengths (and weaknesses). A strength is something that you naturally do well—it just flows. Knowing the strengths your employees have is very valuable, because you can help them put those strengths to work—very satisfying for your workers. This also becomes useful for putting together a well-rounded, functional team (see Part Three, Perfect Phrases for Caoching Teams). A weakness is, obviously, something that a person doesn't do very well, for whatever reason—it just doesn't come naturally. Sometimes, a weakness is a strength taken to an extreme, such as an excellent communicator who tends to gossip or dominate a conversation.

- What are some of your strengths?
- What are some of your skills?
- How do you like to put your strengths and skills to work?
- What kinds of tasks come easily for you? What do you enjoy doing?
- When you're at your best, what are you doing?
- What are some of your weaknesses?
- How do you cope with your weaknesses?
- How can I support you in being your best?
- If you could pick one area to focus on for improvement, what would it be?

There are many professional assessments available for determining strengths, talents, and abilities. Consider using these tools with your employees as a way of getting to the core of what comes naturally for them. It's one thing to say something is a strength, it's another thing entirely to actually put it to use appropriately.

Learning about Working Style

Everyone has a slightly different working style. Some are extremely focused and productive for parts of the day and less effective at other times. Some work steadily and get things done at a reasonable pace. Some folks are quite sociable, others seem more withdrawn. Some panic at small setbacks, whereas others might soldier through to a solution. You can improve employee performance by respecting each person's working style as much as you can.

- What motivates you?
- How do you like to work?
- What is your most productive time of day?
- How do you like to structure your workday?
- How do you handle task management?
- What kinds of things help you focus and stay on task?
- How do you approach handling multiple tasks and responsibilities?
- How do you deal with something that goes wrong?
- What kinds of things distract or bother you?
- Do you need any particular equipment [i.e., ergonomic chair] or accommodations [i.e., desk away from a busy hallway to cut down on distractions]?

Management Needs

Some employees want to work with minimal management guidance or oversight, largely on their own. Others prefer more regular management contact to stay on track. You serve your employees well by not just blindly applying your own management style to them, but by listening and paying attention to how they like to be managed. You can incorporate this knowledge with your own skills and techniques to build a great team.

- How much guidance or management contact would you like at first [daily, weekly, as needed]?

- How should I check in with you [e-mail, casual chats, scheduled one-on-one meetings]?

- I'm here to support you as you do your job. If you need me, here's how I'm available [outline policy/practice/preference].

Chapter 3
Onboarding and Training

The steepest part of the learning curve for a new employee is during the initial training period and immediately after. There is a lot of information to take in when learning about a new company, procedures, policies, systems, methods, and responsibilities. Everyone learns at their own pace, too, so some people will be up to speed relatively quickly; whereas, others need some more time.

Determining the Employee's Learning Style

People learn in many different ways. Some are auditory, preferring to hear information and process it that way. Some are visual, preferring to watch demonstrations. Some learn best by reading, and others are kinesthetic, meaning they prefer to learn by actually doing tasks.

- How do you like to learn?

- How do you learn best?

- How do you like to have information presented to you? How do you process it?

- When you have questions or need help, go to [give names].

- Don't be afraid to speak up, say you don't know, or ask for help. That's what we're here for!

Consider supplementing any standard training materials with various techniques to support the learning style of your new employee.

Delivering Training

Your company might have specific training programs and materials available for new hires. Large companies tend to have more organized, coordinated materials. Keep in mind that this is a lot of information for new employees to process! At first, they will have many questions.

- Our training procedure here is as follows . . . .

- The most important things to learn about your job are . . . .

- Focus on [tasks, skills, procedures, responsibilities].

- Company policies and procedures are important, but not as critical as learning your roles and responsibilities.

- I acknowledge this is a lot to take in, so don't hesitate to ask for clarification or help when you need it.

- You aren't expected to master all of this right away, but we do need you to learn steadily and confidently.

- What questions do you have about the training?

- Let me know how the training experience is for you. Your feedback is important.

Leveraging Peers and Colleagues

Your existing employees are wonderful resources when bringing a new worker on board. Your team members can model appropriate behavior and techniques as well as directly teach and mentor new employees. Connecting new hires with experienced workers creates more engagement for everyone.

- To learn about certain tasks or procedures, I'm going to pair you up with [person] to watch how he does it.

- [Person] is very good to ask about [specific areas of expertise].

- [Person] has agreed to mentor you through this training time, and beyond if you want.

If you have hired several people all at once, and they will be training together, you have a great opportunity for team building as well.

- All of you will be training together, and we encourage you to discuss and learn from each other.

- Your group mentor will be [person].

Providing Constructive Feedback

As a manager or leader, you are responsible for giving feedback to employees. This is critical for new hires, because they are still learning their ways in the organization. A coach approach means that you will keep the feedback positive and constructive wherever possible. You might find the opportunity to give feedback at formal meetings, such as at the end of training or the probationary period. You'll also have chances for giving feedback at more casual one-on-ones as your new worker comes to ask questions.

- You did very well at [task]! Keep it up!

- You're definitely on the right track, keep at it and you'll be proficient in no time.

- With a little time to practice, you'll get faster at these tasks and they will seem much easier for you.

- You seem to need a little help with [task], so I'm going to support you by [assigning a mentor], [reviewing it personally].

- Your new coworkers have observed you and told me [positive feedback].

- You are tracking well on your duties, and we'd like to see you improving in the following areas [give specific details].

Remember to keep your feedback constructive. If you have to point out something a person did wrong, be sure to offer ways to improve—don't just criticize and leave it there. Share the impact her behavior caused all the way to the client. Be able to demonstrate how her efforts and results align with the greater mission and vision for the company.

Offer feedback by using the "sandwich technique." Give a piece of positive feedback, then give one that might be more negative, and end with another positive note. A specific example: A new employee is responsible for social media content and strategy for a retail clothing chain. "You really picked up our brand message and corporate values quickly! We were impressed with your sample tweets and blog posts. Ensuring our customers see this on a regular basis really aligns with our goal of increasing our brand recognition in the market. You had a few issues with terminology and grammar, so when you've reviewed our style guidelines again, we can go over them together. My team members tell me you have some exciting new thoughts for how we can use emerging kinds of social media, and I definitely want to hear more about that. I'm very pleased about your fresh ideas!"

Finally, you can use open-ended questions to get the new hire's feedback and self-analysis.

- What do you feel most comfortable with?
- Where would you like some help or support?
- How are things going with your coworkers?
- Are our internal policies making sense to you?
- What do you need from me?
- How are you tracking on your short-term goals?
- What do you enjoy most about being here?
- What feedback can you offer for how we might improve your experience?

Some of these questions are designed to open up two-way communication by soliciting employee feedback about the company and acknowledgment makes a big difference in creating an environment of employee engagement.

Offering Reassurance

Newly hired employees need some reassurance that they are doing all right. As I've already pointed out, they are learning everything, from tasks and procedures to corporate culture and office politics. It can be overwhelming, and they often are not sure if they are doing well, doing poorly, or somewhere in between. Your reassurance (in addition to feedback) can be critical for keeping them engaged and building rapport. It doesn't have to be a big deal—a verbal pat on the back in person or in a staff meeting can work wonders.

- You're doing great with the training!
- Particularly, you mastered [task] faster than we had expected.
- You're right on track. It takes most people [how much time] to get up to speed.
- I remember when I first started, I was afraid I wouldn't get it right! But I did, and you will, too.
- We're satisfied [happy, thrilled] with your progress.
- What you are learning and doing will significantly impact our customers. You are going to make a big difference here.

Providng Tools and Resources

Part of being a good manager or leader is knowing what's available to support your employees. What tools and resources do you have to offer them? An employee handbook may have that information buried in it somewhere, but a new employee will be more appreciative if you make the effort to connect him with the proper support.

- Some of the programs you might not know about yet include [list programs, i.e., internal mentorship, professional association sponsorship, wellness program, lunch and learn programs, etc.].
- I particularly think you might benefit from . . .
- What are you interested in taking advantage of?
- What other resources might be useful for you?

Part Two

Perfect Phrases for Coaching Employees

Your employees create the results for the organization. Keeping them performing well is a primary concern for most companies. What matters most to you at work probably matters to your employees as well. It's good to remember that your employees are *people*, just like you. Naturally, they will vary in their productivity from time to time. No one can perform at 100 percent all of the time. They need your support, as well as your understanding and encouragement when things don't go as planned. With your coaching skills to support them, employees might begin seeking and even craving your coaching! This section includes some ideas for knowing your employees, identifies opportunities for coachable moments, and wraps up with suggestions for coaching low-, average-, and high-performing workers.

In addition to knowing your employees, remember to check in with *yourself* from time to time. Ask yourself the same questions you would ask your team members. After all, you are growing and changing in your role and as a person. Something that worked well two years ago might not be as effective today or next year.

Chapter 4
Know Your Employees

Before you can coach your employees, you need to *know* them. As a manager or leader in your organization, you have the unique position of knowing what frontline workers are doing as well as the big picture mission and vision of the company. Every person is different, and your knowledge of your employees is key to being able to coach them well. You need to know what they value, what motivates them, and how they work so you can keep them engaged and productive. What matters most to them ultimately matters to your organization's success and makes the coaching approach and collaboration that much easier.

Determining Employee Strengths

If you have been working with a group of employees for a while, you probably know their strengths and weaknesses. If you have conscientiously worked with new hires and asked them about their strengths, then you know those, too (see Chapter 2, Learning about Them). As a review, a strength is something that someone naturally does well—it just flows as part of who he is. Knowing the strengths of your employees is very valuable, because you can help them put those strengths to work for everyone's benefit. A weakness is, obviously, something that a person doesn't do very well, for whatever reason—it just doesn't come naturally. Sometimes, a weakness is a strength taken to an extreme, such as an overly detail-oriented person who might lose sight of the big picture.

Most individuals don't realize when their strengths become weaknesses, so helping them see themselves in a safe coaching conversation becomes key to helping them adjust and moderate their strengths so they are useful to everyone.

Now and then, you might need to directly ask your employees about their strengths as they see them. This is not just a one-time question to ask when they are hired! Make notes on their responses, and add your own observations after you are familiar with how they work. Here is what you can ask.

- What do you feel are your strengths?
- What do you love doing?
- What are some of your best skills?
- How do you like to put your strengths and skills to work?

- If you could do any part of your job all day long, which part would you choose?
- Which tasks come easily for you?
- What do you enjoy doing here?
- What are some of your weaknesses?
- What don't you like to do?
- How do you support yourself around your weaknesses?
- Where do you go for help when you are required to do work that isn't your strength?
- How can I support you in being your best?

There are several professional assessments available for determining strengths, talents, and abilities. Consider using these tools with your employees as ways of getting to the core of what comes naturally for them. This can be an eye-opening opportunity to optimize everyone's work performance.

Working Styles

People like to work in different ways, and it often parallels their personality traits. A social butterfly might like to take regular breaks to connect with people or excel in communication-related tasks. Others are more introverted and might prefer to work seemingly without much contact with others, even telecommuting or working from home, if allowed. Some people are productive first thing in the morning; others don't really get moving until after lunch. Some are easily distracted, some can focus very well even in the midst of chaos. Helping your employees perform at their very best might mean taking account of and accommodating for their preferred work styles.

Everyone is different. Can you see how you might accommodate the different styles in your team? What barriers can you envision by doing this? What solutions or alternatives might be available to overcome these barriers?

If you've been working with your employees for a while, you have probably deduced a lot about their work styles. But now and then, you might want to check in on how a change might help them improve. You can ask these questions one on one, or in a group meeting if you want to generate broader discussion.

- How do you like to do your work? Be specific.
- What would an ideal day be like for you in your job?
- What is the optimal level of management contact you want?
- How often do you want to be partnered with me or other leaders in the group?
- Are you comfortable asking for assistance and advice? How does that approach serve you best?

- What are your distractions and time-wasters, and how can you keep them to a minimum?
- If we limited the number of meetings we have each week to free up time for work, how might that affect you? Is that something you feel would help or hinder you?
- If we offered a more flexible workday, how might you structure your day to be more productive?
- What tools can we provide to help you with task management?
- How can we help you become focused and stay on track?
- When are you most productive during the week? During the day?
- When are you most fatigued?

A major change in the office can wreak havoc on people's productivity and work style. For instance, moving to a new location, rearranging office layout or other changes to physical space, layoffs and restructuring, new equipment and processes, and natural disasters will shake people out of their routines and force some changes. Even adding a new team member can create a ripple in the dynamics of the team and be seen as a major change. After a major change (and after seemingly minor ones), it can be good to check in with your employees.

- How has this change affected your work style? What's improved, and what has been difficult?
- What's going well? What's not going well?
- If you could change one thing, what would it be? Why?
- What are the new challenges that have arisen for you?
- How are you dealing with these challenges?
- What can I do to help you?

Consider a simple example. In a rearrangement of workspace, a person who used to work in a cubicle by a window now works in a cubicle by an employee entrance. You ask the foregoing questions and find out that he finds the new cubicle to be more physically comfortable (not as warm as by the window, plus there's no glare on his computer monitor). However, because people are passing in and out of the entrance all day, he gets a bit distracted by the noise and sights of coworkers walking by. After brainstorming with you, he decides to move his computer to the other arm of his L-shaped workspace, so that he's not directly facing the door, and he asks permission to use headphones to listen to his MP3 player during the day so he's not as distracted by noises. He also asks for a headset to use with his phone to cut down on background noise when taking client calls, which you agree to order for him.

Asking about Needs and Wants

It pays to check in with employees on a regular basis about their needs and wants. As a person grows in her position and changes as a person, her needs shift. The company may increase, decrease, or change the resources available to her. If you can satisfy the needs of your employees, you create an optimal environment for high performance. When you know their wants, you can help them get motivated to achieve more.

- What do you need to do your job?

- What would help you do it even better?

- What resources do we offer that you want to take advantage of?

- I know that you want to achieve [goal]. Did you know that we offer [a resource or benefit] that can help you?

- Who in the organization do you look up to? Is there anyone you would like to learn from as a mentor or advisor? Perhaps we can make an introduction or find a way for you to do an informational interview, shadow, or create a mentoring relationship with him.

For example, imagine Anna, an editorial assistant at a large publisher. After a year on the job, she has mastered the basics pretty well, and you know she has ambitions to get promoted. During her performance review, you discuss her wants and needs.

Anna tells you that her slightly older computer doesn't have enough hard drive space to store all the files she needs, and she has to archive them more frequently than most people in the department. But then, she needs the files again, and has to re-extract them, which is frustrating and confusing—sometimes she doesn't get the most updated files. She asks for a new computer, as well as an ergonomic keyboard to help alleviate the wrist pain she sometimes has. You agree to order the keyboard and offer a compromise of an external hard drive instead of a new computer, which she accepts.

When you ask Anna about the resources available that she wants to take advantage of, she talks about wanting to attend an upcoming industry conference, where she can learn about state-of-the-art tools and techniques. You agree to look into sending her to this event, as the company will pay some or all of her fees and travel. It's clear she wants to learn more, so you explain to her that the company offers a tuition reimbursement benefit if she takes classes in her spare time. She had forgotten about this benefit, and gets excited when you mention it because she has found some excellent e-learning classes through a university that will help her grow her editorial skills.

After reading this section and example, ask yourself these questions:

- Who in your organization did this story remind you of?
- Where have you had requests from employees for additional training or exposure?
- What comes to mind as an opportunity to support your employees in self-development and increase skill development?
- What resources does your company offer in support of such requests and experiences? In house? Out of house? Online?

Fostering Employee Engagement

We talked about engagement in Chapter 1, Encouraging Engagement, when you were onboarding new hires. It bears some emphasis here as well, because continued engagement is important to a thriving workplace. An engaged employee is one who is excited about, invested in, and involved in the work (the mission, the vision) of the organization. Research has found that companies with highly engaged employees more than doubled revenues compared with less engaged companies. The effort you put in to encourage engagement can have big dividends.

Engagement isn't about giving your employees lots of perks or benefits to keep them happy. It is about aligning what matters most in their lives—their values—with the greater vision and mission of your organization. When workers feel this connection and alignment, they will want to go above and beyond; they will eagerly commit to new initiatives and projects. They will jump on board fully to ensure the organization, the team, and you make it around the next corner even when they don't know what is coming next. You can begin helping employees renew their sense of engagement most any time with some key, pointed questions to help them make a personal connection to the bigger picture.

- How do you see what you do (and what you've done) as contributing to this company?
- Can you draw a straight line from your work to the ultimate customer/client experience?
- Why do you believe we, the company, do what we do?
- How do you see your role in this department? What do you think of the work we do?

- Why do you do your work? Why do you come to work every day?
- It's been a while since you started working here. Do you feel your perceptions of this company have changed?
- Is this job what you expected? Does anything exceed your expectations? Did we fail or fall short in meeting any of your expectations?
- How do you see your role in our industry? What contributions are you making?
- You've grown, personally and professionally, in your position here. How has that affected you?
- The [company, department, industry] has changed a lot over the past few years. How has that affected you and your work?
- What do you love about your job?
- What do you wish you could have more of, do more of, experience more of?
- How has being a part of our team helped you grow? Why?

Chapter 5
Performance Review

What is the reason for a performance review? Pause long enough to remind yourself of the intent of providing feedback to your employees, and you will help ease the process for identifying the most productive review. Many organizations hold performance reviews on a regular basis (often annually). Whether or not there is a formal process for this, you should take advantage of the opportunity to help your employees learn from the past and set goals for the future.

When you get your own review, make good use of it for your personal goals, too. Take it seriously and ensure you've given yourself the time you deserve to focus on your own career. Knowing how a powerful performance review looks and feels for yourself will make your experience with your employees even better. Performance reviews are very good coachable moments. Let's see how you can apply coaching skills at every step of the way.

In a good performance review, you'll be sharing feedback with the employee and eliciting it in return. This is a great opportunity to renew the sense of engagement and motivation for a worker. Go beyond the list of "what was good, what was bad" and create a powerful moment to inspire growth and learning.

Giving and Receiving Feedback

Feedback is absolutely critical for employees to know what they are doing right and what needs improvement for them to be successful and meet their goals. Without this input, employees may not know what they are doing correctly or what is working well and won't know what to prioritize, fix, or adjust.

Imagine that you're a video game developer, and you're working on coding certain aspects of a new game. You're using a new game engine that is somewhat unfamiliar to you, and you are making do as best you can. Every time you ask your supervisor a question or seek his feedback, he says he doesn't have time to review it. So you keep plugging along, still unsure if your code could be improved or optimized. After a few weeks, your supervisor calls you in and says he has to let you go because your code wasn't up to par, other segments of the game play won't work with your parts, and now the whole project is very behind schedule. Some judicious two-way feedback—from the supervisors, and probably from your peers as well—could have prevented all of this.

You can use open-ended questions to get the employee's feedback and self-analysis about the previous year. If you begin with the employee's thoughts before you get to the feedback you will give, you create an environment in which the employee feels heard and valued. A self-assessment up front gives sufficient time for the employee's thoughts, and allows you to learn a lot and possibly ease the impact of constructive feedback that follows. You may also learn about issues, opportunities, and important insights before getting to the rest of the performance review.

- What did you most enjoy doing this year?
- What went really well for you?
- What did you least enjoy doing?
- What didn't go so well?
- If the past year could have been better, what would have been different?
- How are things going with your coworkers and in the office?
- What has changed for you in the past year? How have you grown? What lessons have you learned?
- Where would you like some help or support?
- Where am I providing you the support you need? Where do you need more support?
- If there is one thing you wish I could do more of, what would it be?
- What do you need from me?
- What feedback can you offer me for how I work with you?

Note that some of these questions in this chapter are designed to open up two-way communication. Soliciting and acknowledging your employee's honest communication makes a big difference in sustaining an environment of employee engagement. When you know what matters most to your employee, you increase your ability to meet her needs and drive the needs of the business and your own as her leader. The goal is to find a way that engages your employee while supporting the goals and mission of the organization.

After soliciting self-feedback, it's time to share your own feedback with your employee. When reviewing the past year's performance, remember to give clear, honest, specific feedback. You want to encourage the behaviors you want to see more of going forward. For example, consider Ali, a top talent employee. He has been in Jeff's organization for about a year. Jeff considers Ali the best thing to have happened to him in ages and is very appreciative that Ali has chosen to work with him and his group. He is always telling Ali, "Keep doing what you're doing" and "You are great, keep it up!" Although Ali is pleased that he is clearly doing a great job, he is disappointed not to have specific feedback about exactly what he is doing that is so great.

- Your hard work was noticed and appreciated this year.
- We particularly liked your work on [project, product, or task].
- Because of your effort, the result was [specific, measurable outcome].
- I notice that you [do something] particularly well, and I appreciate that!
- What do you see as your best work this year? Why?
- I want you to realize that your work in this department really helps us achieve our goals and work in alignment with our company vision.
- I personally appreciate . . .

A great way to offer feedback is to use the "sandwich technique." Give a piece of positive feedback, then give one that might be more constructive, and end with another positive note. (See the following sections: "Acknowledging Good Work" and "Learning from Challenges" for more examples.) There are ways to offer negative feedback or constructive criticism without seeming as if you're finger-pointing or blaming and shaming.

- We saw some improvement from you in [specific issue] this year, and I think you can do even better.

- I'm sure you realize that [specific issue] wasn't your best work. We'll focus on that a bit so we can get past it and on to something better.

- We want you to improve in the following areas: [be specific].

- We had some concerns about [specific problems]. Let's work on that together.

Acknowledging Good Work

We all need a pat on the back now and then. Acknowledging an employee's accomplishments and achievements goes a long way toward keeping people happy and committed. You definitely want to take notice and reward positive behaviors so that you'll see more of them! The good news is that positive feedback is free and easy to do!

The first thing to remember is to be timely and very specific in what you praise. In addition to praising in private, such as during a performance review, consider praising employees in public as well—whether that's in a staff meeting, project completion wrap-up, or even a formal awards banquet. This lets everyone else see the kinds of behaviors and achievements that are rewarded. If public recognition isn't appropriate or isn't possible in a timely manner, pick up the phone or walk to an employee's office and share the recognition with them as close to the event as possible.

- Your work on [project] was outstanding.
- We particularly liked how you [specific action or accomplishment].
- You have really improved this year, and I appreciate your work.
- Your solid work effort has been reliable, and we all count on you!
- Your work really made a difference!
- You went above and beyond what we expected.
- I see that you met all your goals and objectives from the last time we had this review. Way to go!

- I've noticed that you seem motivated and energetic, and it builds up the energy of those around you. Your positivity is really felt.

- We are very pleased to let you know that you earned [an award, a gift, a bonus, a raise, a promotion] this year.

- I just wanted to say, "Thank you!"

Some of these foregoing examples are a little broad; be sure to fill in details with specifics of what the employee did well.

Learning from Challenges

Of course, no one has a perfect year. There are always issues, problems, and sometimes spectacular failures and catastrophes. Sometimes mistakes are completely the fault of the person who committed them. Other times there may be circumstances beyond anyone's control that can wreak havoc. A performance review is a good time to take a look back and discover what can be learned from all of these challenges.

Remember to keep your comments constructive. You want to arrive at a positive, or at least an appropriate, outcome. If you have to point out something a person did wrong, be sure to offer ways for improvement and get their thoughts on this as well. Share the impact their behavior caused, but be careful not to blame the person.

- We had a few issues with [problems], but we can work on them to create some improvement.

- This project went into a bit of a meltdown, as you know. What did you learn from that whole process?

- You were responsible for [task], and it didn't go according to plan. How did that happen?

- How can we prevent these mistakes from happening again?

- How would you like to move forward from this point?

- What do you see as the key learning points from these challenges?

- What do you think might be challenging for the coming year? How will you deal with it?

- How can I support you if these issues occur again?

- If you reflect back on this situation, what do you feel you learned about yourself? Any surprises?

Setting Goals

A major part of most performance reviews is not only to reflect on past results and performance but to set goals for the coming year. You may have predetermined some objectives and goals to challenge your employee to reach. Don't forget to ask about their goals. When workers can align their personal and career goals with the tasks of their jobs, they become invested, motivated, and engaged. Be sure to ask for short-, medium-, and long-term goals.

- Given the company's goals for this next year [or quarter], I would like to challenge you to achieve the following [list goals].

- Our department has some new goals and projects, and here is what we want to encourage you to do to contribute [identify specific tasks and goals].

- We would also like to see you improve your skills in [area].

- How do you feel about the goals we have set for you? What are your thoughts on them?

- What goals do you want to set for yourself in terms of our department's goals and projects? Our company's overall goals and mission?

- What personal goals do you want to achieve within the next three months? Six months? One year?

- What long-term goals do you want to set in terms of your career? What steps will you take toward those goals this year?

- What do you need from me in terms of support for those goals?

- How do you suggest I check in with you on your progress?

How can I hold you accountable for your goals?

■ How will you hold yourself accountable?

Review Chapter 6, Goal Setting, for some more techniques that will help you and your employees set powerful, achievable goals.

Moving Forward

It's one thing to say you want something, and another thing entirely to take action to achieve it. You can talk the talk, and you should walk the walk! After giving feedback and setting goals, lay out a plan with the employee for moving ahead and validating her efforts. This should be a call to action!

- I'm excited about what we've talked about here! I think we'll have a great year ahead.

- I feel even more confident about our goals and objectives now that we've had this conversation. Thank you for participating attentively, sharing, and demonstrating your commitment.

- How do you feel about this review? How do you feel about your work now?

- What are the first steps you plan to take to get started right away?

- Will you commit to these goals and next steps?

- How will you hold yourself accountable to making these commitments?

- Is there anything else you would like to discuss?

- Is there anything you believe I should be aware of that we haven't discussed?

- I'll get to work on the support you need from me.

- In the next few weeks, I'll check in with you, as we agreed, to see how you're doing.

Chapter 6
Goal Setting

A goal is a dream with a deadline. —Napoleon Hill

Goal setting can be the difference between just wanting success and actually achieving it. We all want to be successful, but it is just pie in the sky until we define it, commit to the goal, and get to work. There are several techniques for goal setting that help maximize one's chances for accomplishment. You can apply these when working with employees and help them on the road to success. Their success is your success!

There are constant opportunities for goal setting in the work environment. Obviously, annual or semiannual reviews are very appropriate times to set goals (and check in on previously set goals), as are project or team kick-off meetings. Staff meetings can be a good time to set weekly or monthly goals, as can informal or quick meetings with employees. You can use the following techniques for setting your own goals as well.

Goals should always be positive. We focus on what we want, not on what we don't want. Focusing on what we don't want only brings more of the same, because our attention and energy are on the negative. In tough and unstable times, though, it can be easy to forget this. Sometimes people start goal setting with a laundry list of things they don't want: "I don't want to have a project fail, I don't want to work 90 hours a week, I don't want to travel as often." Sometimes people don't even know what they want because they are so intently focused on what they don't want. You may need to take some time and effort to get them steered in the right direction.

- What do you want? [Repeat as necessary, it might be several times.]
- I respect that you don't want [something]. If you don't want that, what do you want?
- If you want less of something [i.e., frustration], what would you want more of?
- What lessons have you learned from the things you don't want? How can we carry that forward to a positive outcome?
- Let's keep this focused on the positive so we can push our attention and efforts in the right direction.

SMART Goals

You may have heard of the acronym SMART goals. This is a well-known goal-setting technique that puts you on the path to success with a few key steps. SMART stands for specific, measurable, achievable, realistic, and timed.

SPECIFIC

A goal should be as specific as possible. When a person focuses on a specific thing he or she wants, the brain is able to focus attention and intention on it. It also becomes easy to determine whether or not the goal has been achieved. A vague goal like "I want to improve" or "I want more responsibility" is less likely to be achieved. Also, be sure that goals are not just items that are basic job requirements—not what is expected but opportunities to meet key milestones within one's area of responsibility.

- What, specifically, do you want to achieve? What is the goal?

- If we are successful, what will be the result?

- You say you want "more responsibility" [or another vague goal]; tell me specifically what you mean by that.

- At the end of the month [quarter, year], what would you like to have accomplished?

- How will you and everyone else know that you have accomplished that goal?

MEASURABLE

Specific goals are measurable. Specific goals probably have obvious ways to measure them (specificity and measurability go together). For instance, a goal of "increase revenues 20 percent" is measurable if you track the previous period's revenues against the current period's revenues. It will be obvious and undeniable if there is a 20 percent rise. If you cannot measure the outcome, you will not know whether the goal was achieved. Specific and measurable goals allow you to clearly track how you're doing.

It is possible to help someone define a goal that seems totally objective and not measurable, like "I want to be a better speaker" or "I want to be more confident and assertive." In these cases, you can use a scaling question, asking the person to rank themselves in that area on a scale of 1 (low) to 10 (high), and state where they want to be in the future. In that way, the goal is still objective, but is now measurable.

- You want to increase your billable hours [or other quantifiable goal]. By how much?

- How will this change be measured?

- On a scale of 1 to 10, with 1 being "not good at all" and 10 being "excellent," where are you right now in terms of [this area for improvement]? Where do you want to be on this scale?

ACHIEVABLE

Achievable goals are those goals that are within *your* grasp and within, for the most part, *your* control. This is a very important distinction that can really trip people up sometimes. You can only control yourself. You cannot control events that are bigger than yourself or the results of actions of others. It is pointless to make goals like "I want to get my boss to treat me better" or "I want to win the lottery."

- Is this goal within your power to achieve? If not, what is within your power?

- Your goal is not entirely within your control. We can't focus our energy on what we want other people to do or events we want to happen to us.

- We can focus our attention on our own efforts to influence or communicate with others, and we can set ourselves up for success in a situation as best we can regardless of other events that are beyond our direct control. How might you do that in this situation?

REALISTIC

Goals should be relevant and realistic. Setting a goal outside the realm of possibility means you might waste a lot of time and energy struggling to reach it when you can't and maybe enter a shame spiral if you feel like a failure for not achieving it. I might want to be an NBA player starting forward, but given that I'm only five feet tall and fairly uncoordinated, this goal isn't really realistic for me. You are bound by the laws of physics and time. You cannot change the past, as much as you might want to. In addition, realistic objectives should keep in mind any limitations (or, positively, special talents) you might have.

- Think about what you want to achieve, your current resources and abilities, and other factors that might have an affect on the outcome.

- Is it realistic for you to achieve this goal?

- What might be a more realistic approach? Should you make adjustments to your plan?

- What are the minimum and optimum levels of success here? If everything went absolutely perfectly, what would be the result?

A "stretch" goal or a true challenge might be good thing for motivated, hard-working employees, as it can push them to greater heights. Some people really rise to the challenge.

TIMED

The last letter in the SMART acronym stands for "timed" for completion. These goals are to achieved by a specific date. If you don't have a timeline for achieving your goals, you may not get to work right away. It will always seem to be "sometime in the future," and of course we all know that tomorrow may never come. This is also a reason to have a variety of short- and long-term goals. You can track how you're doing frequently instead of making a set of goals and then just forgetting about them.

- What's your timeline for completion?
- How much flexibility do you have in the schedule for completion?
- What are the immediate short-term [medium-term] goals, and when will you achieve them?
- If this goal has phases of completion, how far apart are they spaced?
- Do you need to build in more time to compensate for things that might go wrong?

Contingency Planning

In the zeal of setting exciting goals, we can forget about existing responsibilities or upcoming issues that might affect our plans. It's wise to help your employee do a little contingency planning when setting goals. This can help keep goals realistic and within reach, as well as preventing panic (to a certain extent) when things inevitably go a bit wrong . . . or right! Sometimes things succeed beyond our wildest dreams and we have to make changes to keep up. Imagine selling 100 times more units than were anticipated. How do you meet the demand? How do you ramp up production? What additional resources need to be added?

- How will these new tasks and goals fit with your current workload?

- As you think about the various deadlines and completion dates, do you need to account for any time off? [i.e., business travel, vacation, planned medical or family leave, holidays]?

- What happens if you get sick or injured and need time off or can't function as well as you would like? Who would support you?

- What support systems or backup plans do you [we] need to create?

- What might get in your way? How can you [we] be prepared for that?

- If you get behind, what will you do?

- What limitations might affect your ability to achieve these goals?

- What happens if we succeed far and above these goals?

Defining What Success Looks Like

We often set goals just because we "should" be growing and achieving. Rarely do we take the time to expand our view to think how the bigger picture will be affected. Taking the time to really imagine and visualize success, plus connecting it to some motivating possibilities, can be the key to finding a powerful motivation to action. For instance, someone may set a goal for the next year of bringing in $2 million over last year's sales numbers, thereby getting in position for a big bonus. That person may have the immediate goal of "make more money," but she might have forgotten to connect with what that extra money might let her do that's even more important (buy a home, travel, save for higher education).

You can imagine the successes early in the goal-setting process, or after the initial goals have been laid out. Revisiting the vision of success might be important for maintaining momentum, motivation, and engagement. Also consider celebrating each milestone reached to keep up motivation and positive energy.

- Let's say it's a year [a month, a quarter] in the future, and you've achieved these goals! What does that look like when you imagine it?

- How does it feel to have been successful?

- How would everyone else know you have been successful? How do we celebrate it?

- What does it mean to you to have reached these goals? What does it do for you? Who have you become?

- What does this success allow you to do next?

- Who else is affected by your achievements?

- What does your personal success do for the department? Group? Company? Industry?
- How do your achievements align with the company's mission? With your personal and professional goals?

Identifying Milestones to Measure Progress

SMART goals are timed for completion, and it's even smarter to have checkpoints along the way to success. Breaking down long-term goals into smaller increments helps us get started and stay on task because the smaller pieces are more manageable. It's satisfying to check off items on a list and get some momentum, and this is easier when the tasks are a bit smaller. When coaching employees, help them strategize ways to break their big projects down into smaller ones, with timelines for each.

- With this year-long goal in mind, how should we break it down into milestones?

- What would be reasonable to achieve in each quarter? Each month?

- With that in mind, what are the very first steps you'll take?

- How often should we measure your progress? How should it be measured?

- How often should I check in with you about your status?

Celebrate all the milestones! Encouragement and acknowledgment at each phase can inject new energy into a long project.

- You're really coming along on this project!

- This is looking good, keep up the good work.

- I'm impressed at how you [give specific feedback].

- I can't wait to celebrate with you when it's all done!

- To what do you attribute your success so far? Would you share that with [the team, other individuals] to help us create best practices?

If things have gone a bit wrong, or just not according

to plan, you may need to do some "course correction" coaching.

- What didn't go as planned? How did it affect you?
- What's gotten in your way? How can we deal with that?
- How are things looking now for the goals you wanted? Do we need to adjust anything?
- What have you learned so far that will help the rest of the process?
- What do you wish you would have done earlier, if anything?

Establishing Accountability

Every person is responsible for his or her own actions. This is easy to claim when we succeed, less so when we fail. Beyond simple responsibility is accountability. By encouraging your employees to be accountable for their actions, you help them take ownership of everything they do. Building accountability into goal setting might include letting employees know of the rewards if they succeed and helping them stick to their commitments.

- How can I hold you accountable for achieving these goals? How can you hold yourself accountable?

- How do you want me to remind you of your commitments?

- How should I check in with your progress?

- If you succeed at reaching these goals, you'll be well positioned for [rewards].

If possible, be more specific if you can; for instance, "If you reach this sales target, you will definitely get a promotion" or "If we get this product release back on schedule, then you will be getting a hefty bonus." Only say these things if you are certain the positive rewards will happen or are already in the works. Empty promises will damage your credibility and morale.

With a coach approach, you will definitely stick to the positive whenever possible. The goal is to gain buy-in every step of the way to keep employees motivated. However, if someone has done something to the point that reprimanding or even punitive action may be required, don't hesitate to exercise your authority, if necessary.

Chapter 7
Meetings

Meetings—such as staff meetings, progress updates, team meetings, and even brief check-ins—represent other good coaching opportunities for improved performance, as long as they are done appropriately and with respect to time. Coaching techniques used in a group setting offer you the opportunity to reinforce roles and responsibilities among employees, communicate about expectations, and celebrate accomplishments. You'll also be able to access the synergy of creative thinking that happens when more than one person focuses their attention on something.

In meetings, you can use many of the situational coaching techniques listed elsewhere in this book, such as those for problem solving, goal setting, and team formation (see Chapters 6, 9, and 14). You can be particularly effective at coaching during meetings if you are running the meeting yourself or at least have some sort of leadership position among the attendees. The following phrases and questions should work whether your meeting is in person, over the phone, or online.

Clarifying Roles and Responsibilities

Meetings offer a good opportunity to reinforce roles and responsibilities for employees. In times of change, roles and responsibilities might be very fluid, and some clarity on who does what can be helpful (if not critical). People change, and organizations change; sometimes individual roles and responsibilities must be reshaped, shifted, or recreated.

- As a reminder, [person or position] is responsible for . . . [tasks]
- The procedure for this kind of work is . . .
- As a group, what are we responsible for doing?
- What is each one of us responsible for individually? Who does what?
- How do we create our results?
- How does what we do fit with the rest of this organization?
- Things have been in flux lately. How is that affecting us?
- What changes do we need to make in our roles and responsibilities?
- Who needs support? Who can support them, and how?
- How can we grow as a group?

Finding out your employees' roles and responsibilities from their viewpoints can be quite enlightening. In a fluid, changing work environment, we all tend to wear several hats, and rigid sets of job tasks are not entirely feasible. Getting a reality check on who does what may reveal that what a person actually does may not be aligned with what they are supposed to take ownership of.

Setting Expectations of Behaviors

People are only human, and we don't always exhibit the best behaviors. Occasionally, you'll need to remind your employees of policies and expectations. It's appropriate to do this in a group meeting if the reminders apply to the whole group or if you're trying to help everyone improve. You can use coaching-style questions to engage the whole group and reinforce good behavior. Be sure to note what's going well! If a behavior is negative and limited to a single person, it's best to have a one-on-one meeting to address it. Singling out an employee as a negative example in a meeting can be detrimental to overall morale.

- I am very impressed at how well we are all focusing, even in this time of turmoil!

- I appreciate how you all have come together to get work done [provide specific details if available].

- We've had some issues occurring lately that would be well addressed with a review of our policy . . . [details of policy].

- An issue has been brought to my attention that we all need to talk about.

- What are we doing well and what needs to be improved? How can we make the improvement?

- How do we demonstrate preferred behaviors? I want to see more of . . . and less of . . . .

- How can we challenge ourselves to rise to these expectations?

- Remember what our priorities are . . . therefore, it's important that [desired behavior or goal happens].

- Remember our intention. Therefore, it's critical that [person] perform [duties].

Celebrating Accomplishments

Meetings are a fantastic forum for celebrating accomplishments and achievements. Everyone loves praise, and many appreciate public recognition (others are a bit more shy). Celebrating successes creates a powerful positive environment for more success. Employees feel valued when their contribution are acknowledged. Take advantage of meetings to celebrate accomplishments, from the small to the huge. Whether it's a simple pat on the back or a formal awards ceremony, employees will be inspired to keep on succeeding.

- I want to acknowledge [person's] recent accomplishments! [be specific]
- This award goes to [person] in recognition for . . .
- I'm pleased to congratulate our top performers!
- What are we proud of accomplishing?
- What else can we celebrate?

Chapter 8

Change Initiatives and Working with Employees

It's widely said that the only constant is change. Things are always changing, and frequently we have to cope with unexpected changes that are thrust upon us and are beyond our control. Every day, our choices lead to changes, big and small. Organizations sometimes seek and choose a change and create a focused initiative to make it happen. Big changes can be quite unsettling for employees, especially if they do not see the point of creating the change. As a manager, you are in a unique position to help employees prepare for the change, weather it, and succeed.

Be sure to review Part Four, Using Coaching Techniques with Superiors, which includes some tips on how to use coaching-style questions with upper management. These will be important for working with employees in a change initiative.

Creating a Vision of the Outcome

If you have talked with the leadership team of your organization and know about a change initiative, you hopefully have an idea of what the change is intended to achieve. If they are well thought out, changes aren't made willy nilly. There's an underlying goal in mind, such as increased efficiency, expansion of product line, improved communication, and so on. As a manager, your job will be to paint a specific picture of the desired outcome for your employees so that they can connect their own goals to it.

- We have a big change coming up! In the next few weeks and months, we are going to [outline change in detail].
- The reason for this change is [specific reasons].
- Once this change is in place, we will be able to . . . .
- Remember, our company's mission is . . . . This new change will help us work toward that even better.
- The benefits we will see from this change are . . . .

Let's illustrate these concepts with an example. Allonsy Pharmaceuticals is rolling out a big change: Compensation for salespeople will no longer be based strictly on the number of prescriptions doctors make, but on a whole new paradigm of patient-centered care. Obviously, this is a huge change that makes a lot of people uncomfortable, as they will have to reinvent how they work and report. Bill is the regional supervisor of an eight-state sales area, and he has called a meeting with all 40 of the representatives in this region. He has already attended a meeting at Allonsy headquarters and gotten a clear picture of the change. Bill begins,

> Welcome everyone! You 've probably heard about our new compensation program, which makes some big changes to how we've been used to working. I'm here to give you details and handle questions. First, you should know that there will be a transition phase of six months while we learn to track the new data, make sure we know what we need to know, and get the system moving smoothly. The target date for the final switchover is October 1.

He starts out by sharing some facts and acknowledging that the change is big (and thus probably a bit scary). Bill goes on,

> The reason Allonsy is making this change is to be more responsive and accountable to the patients who need and use our products. The company feels that we need to refocus on our mission, which is, after all, to improve and optimize the health of all people. By moving to a more patient-centered compensation plan, we want to demonstrate our commitment to the people who are helped by what we do. We want everyone to be focused on the patients, so that's why this change is being made.

He has captured, in just a few sentences, the whole purpose of the change and connected it to the company's mission. Bill wraps up the big picture by adding,

> This will mean a major shift in our thinking, and I hope this will make us all more focused in a positive direction. If it weren't for people needing our medications, we wouldn't be here. It's good to remember that. All of you are hard workers, and I believe that this change will not only help us all do better but make us a better company to work for.

Communicating the Effects of Change

Once they have heard the purpose and ideas behind a change initiative, employees want to know how it will affect them.

- This change will affect us in the following ways . . . [be extremely specific].
- Our new procedures will be . . . .
- You will no longer . . . .
- You will still be . . . .
- We are supported in this change by . . . .

In the example of Bill, the regional manager for Allonsy Pharmaceuticals, he lays out how he expects his team to be affected.

Obviously, this major change in our compensation plan will change our procedures! We will be tracking new kinds of data and issuing new reports. You'll still make sales calls on doctors and hospitals as well as hosting educational events for them. You'll still have access to our branded giveaways and limited samples. However, we will now be requiring you to ask different kinds of questions of the doctors, turn in some new reports, and do some new kinds of presentations to different kinds of customers. You won't have to fit so many sales calls in every day, which I know is a relief to some of you! Allonsy is creating the training on the new reports and questions, and we will have a two-day retreat for training and learning. In addition, the company is working on the programs for data analysis to make sure we track the right numbers, and there will be updates to our smartphone app to help you gather and input the right information.

Getting Employee Buy-in

Getting people enthusiastic about a change (or even grudgingly willing) can be quite difficult. Too often, a change initiative simply results in everyone getting a free T-shirt and nothing being really different. Sometimes the perception may be that changes are made just for the sake of making changes, or because there is a new "flavor of the month" that management wants to jump on.

To get buy-in for the change, which will obviously ease its acceptance and increase engagement, you may have to identify key influencers among your employees and target your discussion about the change with them up front. If they are invested in the change, they stand a better chance of getting other employees on board. In addition, they may be more aware of problems and issues that may come up, so you can ask them about what you should be aware of. Think about your team and organization. Who is the biggest influencer? To whom do people turn for help? Approaching this individual before any change can make a big difference.

- What are your thoughts about this change? I would like your opinion.
- How do you think it will affect you? How might it affect others?
- What opportunities does this change open for you? For others?
- What do you hope will happen as this change rolls out?
- How does this change help you grow?
- Where do you see problems or concerns related to this being accepted by the organization?

- What are your concerns moving forward? Who are you concerned about the most?
- How do you see yourself responding as we make this change?
- What advice do you have for me and the rest of the leadership team, before rolling this out?

Back at Allonsy Pharmaceuticals, Bill has a meeting with Malika, one of his high-performing sales reps who is a mentor for several newer sales reps. Malika's opinion is well regarded in his region, and he wants to talk to her about the compensation changes coming up. After some chit chat and coffee, he jumps right in.

Malika, I specifically wanted to talk to you about this change in compensation data tracking. You've got all the facts, and I was wondering what you felt about it.

Malika puts down her mug and looks directly at Bill.

Well, I have to say, it makes me nervous, and I think the other reps are, too. I see why it's being done, and I applaud those reasons. But we are all a bit nervous about whether we'll be facing pay cuts or not get bonuses anymore. It's a bit scary.

Bill responds,

That's a valid concern! I imagine everyone has some fear built up around the implications of this change. I've been assured that pay levels will be held the same during the transition period, and the bonus program will be revamped. Naturally, we want to keep you all motivated! How do you think you might respond during the rollout and switchover? Are you worried about anything in particular?

She says,

I've thought about that. A lot of it will depend on how fast we can pick up the new report procedures. Most of that comes quickly to me, so I'm not terribly worried. I guess it feels a little scary to rely on totally different data to determine how well we're doing.

[Bill] That's fair! It is a bit scary, I agree. But what opportunities do you see this opening up for you and the team?

[Malika] Well, I specifically chose to work for Allonsy because I liked our mission of helping patients. It makes me happy to realize that we will be doing that even more. It's a good feeling! I'm also glad I won't have to jam in eight or ten doctor visits in a day, that gets exhausting. I'm also excited to learn about these new virtual events we will be doing—seems like some cool new skills!

Bill smiles.

It's true, I think we will get to do some exciting new things! How do you think the other reps will respond?

Malika thinks for a moment, then says,

I think you'll get a mixed bag, honestly. Some of us are excited about fewer doctor visits and getting to learn new skills and technology, like I mentioned. But honestly, Bill, you might lose a few reps who just don't want to do this. Some of the folks who just don't know a different way to work, who are entirely dependent on those bonuses, who are really competitive in terms of who sells the most—they might not come along for the ride. That might not be entirely bad for the company, but it would hurt this region for a while.

In a fairly quick conversation, Bill has gotten some very important feedback and insight from Malika. He has helped her voice her connection with the positive aspects of the change, which will help her buy into the benefits.

Encountering Resistance to Change

No matter how big or small the intended change, there will be resistance. Humans are creatures of habit. Just raise the cost of a vending machine soda by 15 cents, and watch the lunchroom riots start. Resistance can run the gamut from quiet muttering to threats to quitting or worse. You will encounter resistance, especially to a really big change, and you need to learn to cope with it while respecting your employees' viewpoints.

Remember, you've had time to process this new plan—once you roll it out, allow your employees time to react, process, and choose their responses. If you listen carefully to the voiced resistance and acknowledge the validity of your employees' perspectives, you will find nuggets of information (beyond just complaints) that can help you smooth the way for the change to go forward. Who knows, you may find even better ways to help your customers.

Anticipate collaboration, and you are more likely to get it. Be there for your team and individuals who are suffering through the change; listen and allow. They will more quickly and calmly come to their choices of action if you are there for them. It takes some time and patience, but in the end is well worth it.

- I understand that you have strong feelings about this change. Let's talk about that.
- How will this change affect you?
- What bothers you about this change?
- What are you afraid might happen?
- What are you really worried about here?

- Can you see any positives that might come along with this change?
- What do you believe is the intent with this change?
- How can I help you during the process?
- This change is going to come, no matter how much we might wish it wouldn't, so what can we do to get ready?
- What will it take for you to be on board with this change?
- What advice would you give me to ensure this transition goes as smoothly as possible?

Let's revisit Allonsy Pharmaceuticals and see how Bill is handling resistance among his team of sales reps. He meets with David, a senior sales rep who has always been successful. David did not seem enthusiastic about the compensation base change at the group meeting, and he seems resentful during conference calls lately.

> David, I get the sense that you don't feel good about this shift to patient-centered data over sales numbers. I want to hear your thoughts on this. What's bothering you about this changeover?

David sighs and fidgets a moment, then says,

> I've been trying to hold my tongue, but it makes me really angry! I've worked very hard and have been very successful, and I feel like this change is going to take all that away from me. It's all going to be touchy-feely instead of based on hard numbers, like prescriptions filled, and I think you're going to stick me with a big pay cut. It looks like my work is going to be carrying those other reps who don't sell as much, and it makes me resentful, frankly.

Bill is not surprised at the vehemence that David displays, but he accepts it calmly.

> You have been very successful, and we are so fortunate to

have you on the team. I can totally see how this entire shift would be frustrating! May I take some time to tell you some more about how the patient-centered approach will be tracked and monitored to drive results that are tangible?

He fills in the details of what data will be examined and how it will determine compensation. David listens, but still seems angry and unwilling to concede anything positive. Bill asks,

How can I help you during the switchover process?

David thinks, frowns, and then says,

> I don't know. I'm not sure I'm going to stay here, to be honest. Other companies would be glad to have me, you know.

> [Bill] I hope you know that we are very glad to have you. We'd like to keep you! Your leadership on this team is as important as the successful results you've always pulled in. I see your leadership and buy-in as an important part of this change. I would hate to see you go. This change is going through, whether we like it or not, so I want to support you as it comes. How can we do that together?

He frowns again, thinks, and then sighs.

> Well, I really do like working for Allonsy. I'd like to stay. I guess I can't stop this change. I'm most worried about learning some of these new reporting procedures and presentation technologies. I know we'll have the retreat, but it takes me longer to pick up new skills like that.

Bill brainstorms with David on how he can help him learn. Notice that this may be the root concern here for David. By creating a safe space and conducting a respectful dialogue, the real fear is uncovered. Bill validates David's fear of being a slow systems and process learner and reassures him that he will get as much assistance as he needs. They agree that Bill will check in by phone once a week during the transition phase, and David agrees to set aside a few hours each week to review the training materials and tutorials. Bill makes a few notes about this plan, so he can suggest it to some other resistant sales reps. He ends by asking,

> So, David, do I have your support and commitment to engaging fully in this change? Is there anything else you'd like me to be aware of to help this be a success?

David gives a rueful chuckle and admits,

> I'm not sure I'll be 100 percent on board, but having a plan for learning the new material is already helping me feel better about the whole thing. I might want to know how bonuses will be decided, so I can use that to motivate myself. You know I'm competitive and like recognition!

In this conversation, David has gone from angry and stubborn to at least a little bit ready to change. Keep in mind that some employees will simply remain angry or stubborn about a change. Some may stir up trouble and need disciplining. Others might go so far as to voluntarily leave the organization.

In the end, the key is the conversation—communications, keeping a two-way dialogue going so you can uncover what really matters most to an employee. The best thing you can do as a leader is keep an open mind, create a safe space for listening and hearing the employee, and check in frequently with questions that validate commitment and accountability to moving forward with the change.

Moving into the Change

As the change approaches and begins, you have the opportunity to check in with your employees and make sure they are staying on board and on track. You still may have resisters at this stage (it's pretty much unavoidable), but hopefully everyone is doing what is necessary to prepare for and facilitate the change. Keeping up encouragement during a time of transition is important for maintaining good morale and keeping everyone on track. One way to approach this need is to remind people of the purpose of the change and desired outcomes. Keep everyone focused on the goal and why it is important to the success of your organization!

■ How are we doing? Are we on track for this change? Are we ready?

■ What is next for us in the change process?

■ What is going well? What is not going so well?

■ What else do we need to do to be prepared?

■ How can we feel good about this change?

■ How can you feel committed to this change?

■ How can we stay committed to this change?

■ How could we make it even better?

■ I have great confidence in our abilities to meet this challenge!

■ It's confusing and sometimes scary to face this kind of change, but I know we can do it.

■ Since there is no going back now, what will you have to let go of to commit to this change?

■ We need your buy-in and engagement. What would that take?

- Remember, the whole purpose behind making this change is . . . .

A few weeks before the change in compensation data at Allonsy, Bill is holding his monthly team meeting. Part of his agenda for the meeting is to check in about the change initiative.

Folks, as you know, we're much closer to tracking the new patient data instead of sales numbers. It's moving ahead as scheduled. I've talked to most of you individually about it, and you've been through some of the preliminary training. I want to find out how you're feeling right now. Are you on track and ready?

Malika smiles and nods, David grimaces a bit, and the others are a mix of positive and negative expressions. There's a bit of muttering, and a few people speak up.

I'm as ready as I can be, just waiting on the next round of training.

I'm excited about the new presentations we'll do!

I'm nervous that our pay will be cut.

The group talks about some of these issues a bit, and Bill sets their minds at ease about the pay being held the same for a while. He says,

I understand that this big a change can be scary! I have confidence in our abilities to rise to the occasion and grow. I want to remind all of you that the whole purpose of this change is to focus on patients, which is our company mission. This will allow us to keep them at the center of all we do, from drug development all the way to marketing and sales.

There are murmurs of assent, and Bill continues.

Well, the shift is coming, and the date is set! We can't

change that. So how can we feel good about it?

It's an unexpected question, and there is silence for a moment. Malika pipes up,

> I don't know if this helps, but I find it kind of exciting to be doing things in a new way! We are going to create and define whole new ways to sell—we can be industry leaders here!

Several other people nod in agreement. David then chimes in,

> I was really against this at first, but the initial rounds of training have been helpful. I'm hoping the retreat will make us all feel confident with what we have to do.

After some more positive comments, including a specific thank you to David, Bill wraps up the discussion.

> Folks, I like what I'm hearing. I'd like us to stay committed and I challenge each of you to rise to the occasion and lend a hand to each other, even if it is just a word of encouragement during the frustrating parts. I think our region can set the standard for the rest of the company! Let's show them how it's done!

Chapter 9
Problem Solving

No job, no task, no day is completely problem free. We deal with countless minor problems all the time. Problems become sticking points when their effects are big enough to be noticed. Sometimes they snowball, creating more problems as they go along. This chapter is about a coach approach to problem solving. (Note: This chapter is really appropriate for handling small to medium problems. For dealing with major crises, review Chapter 10, Coaching Employee Performance after a Crisis.)

An overall principle to keep in mind about problem solving is to stay focused on the solution. Many coaches practice solution-focused coaching, which looks more to creating the desired outcome than dwelling too much on the problem itself. Try to avoid placing blame or pointing fingers.

Identifying and Defining the Problem

You might have an idea of what kind of problem an employee is bringing to you. You might know about a problem before anyone else does. Or you could be completely unaware of trouble brewing. In any case, you should take the time to clearly define the problem. Only then can you focus on the solution you want to come out of it.

- What, exactly, is the issue here?
- What happened (or didn't happen)?
- Where were the breakdowns in the process?
- What are the results and ramifications?
- What has changed as a result of this problem?
- Who else is affected?
- What is happening now?
- What do we want to happen?
- What would be an optimal solution?
- What would be the absolute best result?
- What's our goal?

Validation and Respect for Employees

A key step in listening to employees who come to you with problems, as we have discussed in previous chapters, is to create a safe environment for a dialogue and validation and respect for their viewpoints. You can validate their feelings without agreeing with them or expressing sympathy or pity, which might be misplaced. Employees want to feel heard, and you can foster respect by acknowledging their opinions on the matter at hand. Keep in mind your goal as a coach leader, and move them forward to a solution.

- I understand that you are frustrated and maybe angry [or however the employee feels]. It's natural to feel that way.

- I respect that this problem is an issue for you. Let's tackle it together.

- Your viewpoint is important, and we can't come to a solution without it!

Empowering Employees to Create Solutions

A colleague of mine is constantly turned to when her co-workers can't figure out a problem. Instead of just giving them the answer, she always asks, "What have you tried so far?" A simple question like this puts the power back into the hands of the questioner. They eventually get the message to fend for themselves or, in coaching terms, hold themselves accountable for the work at hand. They learn to only come to her with a difficult question, after they have tried things themselves.

The goal is to have self-empowered and engaged employees to move the organization forward toward its goals. Empowering your employees will give them confidence, let their inner strengths come through, and help them work smarter.

Pause for a moment and notice where you do this well. Where might you have an opportunity to do this more? With which employees? Consider that the more you encourage self-leadership and empowerment within your employee group, the more time you will have to do the work you are being asked to do.

■ What have you tried so far? What were the results of that?

■ Have you dealt with this before? What did you do then?

■ Do we have any procedures or guidelines that might support us?

■ What occurs to you to try? What does your gut instinct say?

■ If you were me, what would you advise in this situation?

■ Who else have you collaborated with? Asked? Partnered with?

Brainstorming for Solutions

Minor issues and problems are frequently resolved fairly quickly. More moderate problems, things you haven't encountered before, may require some fresh thinking and new ideas. Brainstorming is a terrific opportunity to use coaching-style questions. First, figure out the solution you'd like to see.

Before beginning a brainstorming session, identify it as such. Remember, in brainstorming sessions, all ideas are equally accepted as possibilities and captured for consideration. Some ideas may be more obvious than others, but in any case be sensitive not to "shoot down an idea" before the dialogue is complete. Creating a safe space for innovative ideas, lessons learned, and suggestions will help brainstorming be successful when looking for solutions.

- Who cares about this situation being solved? Who are the stakeholders?
- Has anyone ever handled this kind of problem before? What did they do that we could do?
- What skills and strengths can we bring to bear on this problem?
- What resources can we draw on for support?
- How do we create the solution we want to see?
- Why is this important to us?
- If we had all the resources we needed, what would we do? How would that idea solve this problem? Why would we do that?
- How can we do better in the future?
- How can we prevent this from happening again?

Learning from Problems

To move forward, a person needs to learn from his mistakes and problems to be able to grow and change. Make sure you help your employees find the silver linings in their problems as a way to move forward.

- What did you learn as a result of this problem?
- What needs to change because of it?
- If we could mistake-proof this process going forward, what might we do?
- What did you, personally, learn about yourself?
- How were you affected, and how did you respond?
- What could you have done even better in that experience?
- What would you do next time now having had this experience?

Creating a Positive Outcome

Creating a positive outcome from a problem is not just a matter of "spin." It's how we give meaning to what happened and take it from "problem" to "opportunity." Let's be clear here: Negativity and suffering usually come from our perceptions. If we see something as a problem, we experience it as such. If we make a conscious effort to define a situation as an opportunity, it is handled as such. Your role as a manager is key here—you must be the first to decide how a group or individuals will best be supported by choosing your own reaction and response accordingly. You already began some of this when looking at the key learnings. Take it a few steps further to create something positive to move forward so you can lead your employees in the most productive direction. This begins with you.

- Now that we find ourselves in this situation, what were the good things to come out of this? What positive things does it lead to?
- How did we grow stronger? How are we better now?
- What do we need to do to be even better in the future?
- What and who else might be affected by our choices as we move forward?

Addressing Employee-Generated Problems

Employee-generated problems occur because of people's choices and behaviors. Examples of these kinds of problems include mistakes and errors in the work process, task management problems, poor decision making, gossip and drama, communication issues, and so on. The problem may be limited to a single employee (i.e., a worker who spends too much time goofing off online or someone who is constantly late for work and meetings) or a whole group (i.e., breakdowns in communication slowing down a team's project timeline).

Your perception of employee-generated problems is powerful, especially when discussing the problem with others in your organization. Timeliness will be key here, so finding a way to immediately address the issue with the employee involved first, gaining all the facts will be very important to moving forward.

Here are some specific phrases for dealing with employee-generated problems.

- If the issue starts within us, then the solution is within us, too.

- How did the problem start?

- Who else is affected?

- What choices had an effect?

- What can you do to improve or fix the issue?

- You are responsible for your actions, including working toward the solution. Having said that, what do you need from me to help you address this issue?

- What's a fresh way to look at or think about this situation that might offer us some insight?

- What would someone outside this department think about this?
- What information should we provide to others regarding this situation?
- What do other people in this industry do in a situation like this?
- Who else has had this experience? Can we call on them for assistance?
- Is there anything else about this situation you believe I should be aware of before we move forward?

Addressing Externally Generated Problems

Things will happen to you, and there is no control or choice involved. These are externally generated problems, and there is an infinite list of events that can happen to create problems. External problems include things like a supplier not delivering on time, a power outage, computer virus, weather, clients changing their minds, and so on.

- It was not our fault that [external problem] happened. How we respond is within our control.

- What and who were affected by this problem?

- What else came into play that had an effect here? What choices did we make that might have made this better or worse?

- What did this cost us? What would it cost us if it happens again?

- What procedures or policies do we need to put in place to prevent or deal with this?

- What changes do we need to make to move forward?

- What do we need to let go of to move forward?

- How can we get back in control? Realistically, what *can* we control in this kind of situation?

- Who are the key stakeholders who need to be informed about this situation, and what information do they need to feel confident we are moving forward in a solution-oriented manner?

Addressing Industry Changes

It can be almost earth shattering when industrywide changes are brought to bear on an organization. New laws and regulations can have massive impacts. New procedures, practices, techniques, and technology can have big effects as well. Some industries experience constant growth and change, and employees must work hard to stay current and keep up. The good news is that changes large enough to affect a whole industry are often known about well in advance, so there is some time to prepare and plan.

- How does this industry change affect our company?
- What will we need to do differently (or do away with, or create from scratch)?
- How will an individual employee's job change?
- How can we prepare for this coming change? What needs to be in place?
- How can we make the most of this change?
- What do we need to do to take this change in stride and stay productive?
- What other industry changes are coming our way?
- How can we get away from playing catch-up with these changes and move to being a trendsetter and industry leader? What best practices can we already point to?

Chapter 10
Coaching Employee Performance after a Crisis

P roblems crop up every day in the business world. Some are minor and dealt with immediately. Others are more lingering and have deeper effects. Some are catastrophic. Single, well-defined, notable events (e.g., layoffs or a fire) can have deep impact, but so can long-range trends that aren't as urgently noticeable but still have a big effect (e.g., decreased sales over a year or product recalls). We can't always predict a crisis or its severity, but we can almost always learn valuable lessons and create lasting change from it. In some cases you have an opportunity to start over, allowing you to improve in areas you will wish you could have implemented prior to the crisis.

This chapter talks about how to investigate what went wrong (without placing blame), crystallize key learnings, take responsibility, chart a new path, and grow. Note that these conversations should really be had *after* the crisis. During a crisis, most of us are in a "survival" or "fix it now!" mode. Immediately after, people often want to indulge in finger pointing to place blame and responsibility. These are not good opportunities for coaching better performance.

The techniques in this chapter can be used during one-on-one conversations, staff meetings, or team meetings. Be in tune with your employees so you can be sure they are ready to move forward. You can start with some basic statements.

- We're here to talk about [issue].
- We will talk about what went wrong, but we're mostly going to focus on how to move forward.
- I understand that many of you may be frustrated, if not angry, about this situation.
- For now, set aside your frustrations, and let's have a productive conversation about where we go from here.
- Do we all understand where we are and what needs to be done?
- Are there any questions?
- Do I have your commitment to working through this?

Investigating What Went Wrong

It is entirely possible to examine what went wrong while not pointing fingers. You will have to focus more on the how (process) than the why (or the who), and keep your employees focused on this as well. This may require some redirecting now and then. Again, this kind of conversation should be held once any strong negative emotions from the crisis have cooled off.

- How did this happen?

- Where were the breakdowns?

- Remember, placing blame isn't our purpose right now. I'm less worried about who did what, and more concerned about how things didn't go as planned.

- Was this crisis something that should have been anticipated in any way? What signs did we miss?

- Is this something that could happen again? How do we prepare for it?

- Who are the key stakeholders in this process or situation?

Lessons Learned from a Crisis

Some leaders say that there is no failure, only opportunity to learn. This can be the silver lining to the cloud of a crisis. If you take the effort to learn the valuable lessons, you can position yourself for greater success later. Those who don't learn from failures will keep making mistakes. Sometimes the lessons are simple, sometimes they are multifaceted.

Tapping into your employees for key learnings after a crisis will offer you a broader variety of viewpoints than just your own. It also demonstrates to your team that you value their input and thoughts, a vote of confidence that can boost morale after problems.

- So what did we learn from this crisis?
- What can we do to prevent this from happening again?
- If it happens again, how do we deal with it? How do we prepare for it?
- What needs to change because of this crisis?
- What positive lessons came out of this that we can take forward?
- How well did we deal with this problem?
- What went right in this situation?
- How did people go above and beyond to get us back on track?
- How are we better for having weathered this trouble?
- Who else needs to be informed of this situation and what we've learned?

Taking Ownership and Responsibility

Invested, intelligent employees might take responsibility and ownership of their mistakes (if they aren't fireable offenses). No one likes to shoulder blame, or even admit to a serious error. Some people will get extremely defensive and even angry rather than admit a mistake. "Ownership" in this sense doesn't necessarily mean accepting blame or responsibility. Some people may claim ownership of innovative problem solving that helped the situation. Everyone can be encouraged to take ownership of any new changes and responsibilities growing out of a crisis.

- What do you take responsibility for?

- When you think of how you handled this crisis, what are you proud of?

- What are your areas for improvement and growth as a result of this crisis?

- How did this crisis make us stronger?

Forging a New Path

To learn from failure, we have to apply the lessons learned to chart a new path toward success. You've already talked about key learnings with your employees, and hopefully strategized about what to do if the problem turns up again. Every learning experience is an opportunity for growth. With some key questions and phrases, you can turn the lessons learned into action for a more positive future.

- What's next for you? What's next for us?
- We learned some important and valuable lessons. How do we move forward with them?
- How can we apply what we've learned in other areas?
- Let's think about our existing projects and other goals. What needs to be adjusted because of this crisis?
- How can we be better in the future?
- What do you commit to doing as we move forward?

Chapter 11
Coaching Low Performers

Beyond situational coaching and taking advantage of coachable moments, you need some tools for coaching various kinds of performers. Probably the most stressful kind of people to coach are the low performers. For whatever reason, these employees just aren't producing as much as is expected of them. Perhaps they were once good performers and have slipped; perhaps they aren't engaged in the work and don't care very much; perhaps they just don't fit very well in the organization. This chapter will help you clearly outline consequences of low performance, get at the root causes, lay out expectations, create a performance plan, and hold your employees accountable.

Before beginning to coach your low performers toward improvement, ask yourself the following questions:

- What do I know and what have I noticed about this employee?
- What issues do I know about that affect this person's performance?
- What is the minimum I expect from this employee? What is the optimum? What would be ideal?

When you can answer these questions, then you are well prepared to be a true support to someone who might be struggling. For instance, if you know that an employee has done well in the past but has had some chronic health issues lately, you can be empathetic while still encouraging her to improve because you know she is capable. You'll also have a more realistic idea of what is possible for her and how you might offer support (i.e., flex time, medical leave, an assistant) to help her get back on track.

Let's use an example to illustrate these concepts. Marian is a registered nurse who works at the hospital on a 12-hour day shift. Her supervisor, Jill, notices that Marian frequently seems to be running behind and leaves quite a few unfinished tasks for the night shift, which has resulted in complaints from her coworkers. Several informal conversations with Marian haven't improved the problem very much.

Before talking to Marian, Jill thinks about the situation. She realizes that there are two main areas where she wants Marian to improve: updating charts and medication delivery. Marian used to be very conscientious about updating charts, but that seems to have changed since the hospital went to totally electronic record keeping. Her medication delivery also used to be right on time. Jill also knows that Marian gets frustrated easily and lets that affect her work quality. Knowing these things about her employee puts Jill in a positive, constructive frame of mind, which will help her as she coaches Marian.

Setting Expectations for Performance

Do your employees know and understand what is expected of them? When they were first hired, they may have been told what they were supposed to do. With regular performance reviews, they have goals and objectives set. Even so, some employees forget (or never knew) what was truly expected. Expectations might differ from setting goals and projects—for instance, an expectation might be to arrive for work each day by 9 a.m., something that isn't really suited to a long-term goal. It's best to be very clear and direct about what you need each employee to do. Be extremely specific and use measurable terms for assessing performance.

- Your productivity has been lower than I would like. I want to help you improve it.
- The specific areas in which I see room for improvement are . . . .
- At a minimum, you are expected to . . . .
- Optimally, we would want you to . . . .
- Your current level is . . . .
- Obviously, the gap is . . . . Let's work on that together.

Keep the conversation focused around facts as much as possible. It can be very delicate to tell someone that they aren't doing well—many see it as a personal attack. Use facts and numbers wherever possible, and keep the conversation focused on the goal of improvement (less on pointing fingers on what went wrong). You'll have a chance to get at root causes later.

Marian and Jill have a sit-down meeting in Jill's office to address Marian's underperformance.

> Marian, we need to talk about some of the productivity issues that have come up. You seem to run behind frequently, and I think we can help get you on track.

Marian seems a bit angry, but responds,

> Yeah, okay. I do my best, you know, it's a lot to keep track of!

Jill responds,

> That's true! Believe me, I know, I've done it before. We have certain expectations of the nurses on this floor, and I want to be very clear about those, so we can see how you're doing. First, we expect you to finish all your charting before the end of your shift. I looked at your charts for the past week and saw that 8 out of 20 were not updated at end of your shift. Second, we expect a window of no more than 30 minutes from the time a medication order is given and the time it is delivered. Over the past two weeks, I calculate that you averaged a 45-minute delay. These are issues that are quite fixable, if we work on them.

Jill has given very specific instances of expectations and how Marian is stacking up. She has hard data to back up her point. Marian still feels uncomfortable with the whole conversation, but she is listening.

Discussing Consequences of Low Performance

You need to be direct and clear when discussing expectations, and the same goes for outlining consequences. Obviously, you should discuss any negative consequences that might occur as the result of low performance, but be sure to mention the positive rewards that come with improvement. You should also be clear about who and what else are affected by one person's performance. Sometimes, seeing the big-picture vision of one's actions and choices allows an employee to get a wake-up call that can help motivate a positive change.

- When your performance isn't where it needs to be, here's what happens around you . . .
- Other people affected by it include . . .
- We are giving you a chance to improve. If you don't improve, here is what will happen . . . [be specific without sounding threatening].
- We have incentives if you rise to the challenge. If you improve, you will be rewarded with . . .
- We want to see you at a more optimal level of performance by [date].

Again, although it can be a challenge, try to keep your voice neutral and your words focused on facts and procedures. Simply presenting negative consequences ("do better or you'll be fired") may inspire a jump in productivity, but it is based on fear. In response to perceived threats, many employees get defensive, refuse to truly listen, and may even walk out or quit. Finding a more positive way to move forward can help the person feel more motivated. Let's return to Jill and Marian's conversation. Jill has laid out expectations and clearly stated how Marian's performance measured up. She goes on delicately,

> I'm not sure if you're aware of what happens when charts aren't updated correctly. The next shift needs to know what has happened with each patient, so we can have uninterrupted care, and it's not enough to just tell them what you did. We must have everything documented for legal and insurance requirements. The night nurses have their own tasks to do, and picking up a previous shift's tasks just adds to their burdens.

Marian snorts and says,

> They're just lazy, and they complain all the time.

Jill gently says,

> They work 12-hour shifts just like you do, Marian. Nobody likes to pick up unfinished work from the previous shift. Believe me, I'm talking to some other nurses on both shifts who need some help with charting, so I'm not just picking on you. As for the medication delivery time, I think you know the consequences of that. Fifteen minutes off the window doesn't seem like much, but for some of these patients, it can make a big difference in their treatment. If meds aren't delivered at the right time, it can throw off scheduled procedures later. Patient care is our number one priority, as you know, so it's important to work on this.

Marian scowls and looks at the floor. She doesn't make a response. Jill goes on.

> To be clear, I need you to know what will happen if we don't see an improvement. I'd like to see you performing better by the end of the next month, and I'll be checking your charts to see how you do. If things don't change, I'll have to put a written reprimand in your personnel file. If there is no change a month after that, our policy states that you will

rotate to the bottom of the assignment pool, meaning you won't get your top choice of days to work. If there is still no change, we would look at several options, including reducing the numbers of shifts you work, transferring you to a different department that doesn't rely on these same procedures, or even, in the extreme, letting you go.

Marian is shocked and says,

Well, why don't I quit right now?! Sounds like you'd be happier if I left!

Jill stays calm.

That's not true; we want you to do better. Let me tell you the positive side of improving, okay? If you reach the levels we set by the end of next month, I'll write a commendation letter that will factor in heavily when loyalty bonuses are calculated. If you keep your performance at that level, you'll get closer to the top of the assignment pool and be able to have first choice for the days you want to work. If you keep your performance up in the long run, then you put yourself in line for the next round of raises and promotions.

Uncovering Root Causes and Insights

After explaining expectations and consequences, it's time to get at the heart of the matter and discover the root causes behind an employee's poor performance. If you can identify the issue and address it, the employee is on the path for improvement and success. Look for questions that help the employee identify things within his control (review Chapter 9, Problem Solving, for more ideas). They may be tempted to blame everyone and everything else, rather than admit fault, so you might have to gently direct them to look within without placing blame. Here are some phrases you can use, depending on the situation.

- What do you see as the core of the issue here?
- In the past, you were a good performer. What has happened to change that?
- You have made some improvements, but seemed to stall at this level. What caused that?
- What do you think is stopping you from performing well?
- What things are different for you now, compared to when you started working here?
- What affects your productivity levels?

You might be surprised at responses to these questions. In the best case, the employee will take an honest look at his own self and be willing to think about the issue in terms of what he can take responsibility for. Some employees might respond by listing personal problems that you didn't know about (be wary if you think they are offering this as an excuse rather than an issue to cope with). Others might confess true dissatisfaction and desires to leave their positions.

I've mentioned it elsewhere, and it bears repeating here: It is possible to validate your employee's feelings and viewpoint without necessarily condoning or agreeing with her. When you're getting at root causes of low performance, there might well be some negative emotions that rise up. You can acknowledge that these feelings are natural, which can set your employee at ease.

- Anyone in your situation would feel that way, that's natural!
- It's understandable that you would get frustrated.
- We all do the best we can with what we have.

If we revisit the discussion about Marian's low performance, we find that Jill is ready to get at root causes after laying out expectations and consequences. She asks,

Marian, what do you see as the main issue here?

Marian bites her lip, then bursts out,

I hate the new electronic charting! I thought I understood how to do it, but it never seems to do what I want it to. I try to chart, but it won't save my instructions, or I can't find the right menu option, and then I get frustrated, so I walk away to cool off, and before I know it, shift's over and I didn't get it done. It slows me down all through the shift, and I think that's why I don't get to the meds on time.

She seems a bit shocked by her outburst, but also a little relieved.

Jill nods and says,

Oh yes, that was a big change for all of us! It's understandable that you would feel that way—I think we have all been frustrated at times. I'm glad you told me this, because it's definitely something we can work on together.

Crafting a Performance Plan

Now that you've identified the problem or the source of the low performance, it's time to get to work. Craft a plan of action with your employee that will get his performance up to the levels you agree to. Ask questions that put the responsibility in the hands of the employee. (Be sure to review Chapter 6, Goal Setting, and use the techniques and phrases listed there.)

- We've identified the root cause of this issue, and discussed where we want your productivity levels.
- What are you going to do to improve?
- What are the steps you can take immediately?
- What changes will you make?
- Is there someone who is good at the same thing you're trying to improve? What does that person do that you could do?
- What do you need provided to you so you can improve?
- How should I support you?

Look for the worker to make commitments to take action (or, in some cases, stop certain behaviors). Be ready to offer any available resources that might assist her—for instance, if an employee has a sick relative, she might need to take family leave to care for them, but is unaware that this option exists.

Jill and Marian have been talking about Marian's low performance, and she identified her confusion with the electronic charting system as being the main issue. Now they start brainstorming about how to improve.

Jill says,

Marian, what are you going to do to improve?

Marian thinks for a few moments, then asks,

> I'm not really sure. I just get so frustrated! I guess I need some time to figure it out, but there's already too much to do in a shift, I don't see how I'm going to add this to my pile.

Jill nods and says,

> Would you be willing to come in on a day when you're not on the schedule and put in some time training on the system? We have three new nurses starting next week, and you can join them for the session on electronic charting.

Marian grimaces a bit and says,

> Well, I really love my days off, and I have limited time with my kids, but it sounds like I need to get better. Yeah, I can come in, I guess, as long as it's not the whole day. How long would it be?

Jill smiles and says,

> I think we can schedule that part of the training for a two-hour block. I appreciate your willingness to come in! What else might you do to get better?

She thinks a moment and says,

> Well, it seems that Cathy is really good at electronic charting. She's a whiz at it! Maybe she can show me her tricks.

> [Jill] That's a good idea! I can ask her to show you what she knows, or you can shadow her a bit on your next shift together.

With a few key questions and brainstorming together, Marian has come up with a plan of action for her improvement. She and Jill hammer down some of the remaining details and she agrees to get to work on improving.

Creating Accountability

After getting a plan of action in place, you should take the time to establish how your employee will be held accountable. If you've already explained the consequences of low performance and the rewards of improvement, she will hopefully be motivated to change. Some work on accountability can help keep her on track.

■ How will you make sure you stick to this plan?

■ Will you commit to improving?

■ How can I help you hold yourself accountable?

■ What might get in your way, and how can we deal with it?

■ How will we know you have met your goals?

Jill and Marian have come up with some great ideas for improving Marian's performance issues. Jill asks,

Okay, we have a plan in place, so how will you make sure you stick to it?

Marian, says,

Well, I just gotta do it, right? I really do want to have more choice in shifts and I am sort of counting on that loyalty bonus. That's very motivating!

Jill smiles and agrees.

Definitely! How can I help hold you accountable? I'll be monitoring the charting schedule, but do you want me to check in with you periodically?

Marian replies,

Yes, actually, that would be good. If I report to you every other day, I'll probably stick to it.

Jill makes a note to check in regularly. She asks,

What might get in your way? What kind of things might slow you down?

Marian thinks for a moment and says,

My own frustration slows me down, mostly. I'll try to remember to take a few deep breaths when I'm feeling angry!

Jill says,

That sounds good! Finally, let me ask this: When you bring your performance up to expectations and reach your goals, how will we all know you have succeeded?

Marian grins a bit,

Well, I'll definitely be happier, which you'll notice. And hopefully, you'll see me all tan from the vacation I'm going to take with that bonus!

Jill laughs and says,

Sounds great! All right, I'll get back to you with the training session details, and I'll talk to Cathy about you shadowing her a bit.

Chapter 12
Coaching Average Performers

Most employees fall in the middle of the bell curve of productivity. You'll have some low performers, and some high performers, and the bulk will be "average." In modern times of budget cuts and being forced to do more with less, many leaders are keen to take average performers and turn them all into superstars. Competitive workers strive to do better and better, whether they measure their performance against each other or seek to improve on their own work in the past.

Before beginning to coach your average performers, ask yourself the following questions:

- What am I comparing this person with to determine that he is performing at an "average" level? (other employees, company expectations, or prior performance)
- What do I know and what have I noticed about this employee?
- How can I challenge him to rise higher?
- What motivates this person?

When you can answer these questions, you will be prepared to coach someone to go from "good" to "great." For example, if you know an average worker is highly motivated by external recognition, you can offer him a chance at some of the rewards that your organization offers, which might include certificates or trophies, monetary or gift bonuses, opportunities for advancement, or special training and leadership development.

I will illustrate the concepts in this chapter with an example. Ivan is a graphic designer for a major online retailer. He does his job fairly well, and his performance meets the expectations his manager laid out for him. He's not a superstar, but he shows some promise. His manager, Kevin, wants Ivan to step up and do even better. Before talking with him, he takes some time to ask himself the above questions. He decides the following:

- His performance is considered about average compared with other designers at his level.
- Ivan is good at explaining things to others and seems to enjoy doing so. People seem to go to him when they have questions.
- He's been here a while and has expressed interest in promotions but hasn't had one yet. Perhaps we can motivate him that way.
- I would like to see him take on more of a leadership role, as he seems to handle responsibility well.

Validate and Acknowledge Performance

If you're having conversations about performance with average employees, be sure to affirm what they are doing well. We need to praise the behavior we want to see more of. Everyone likes a pat on the back and positive feedback.

- I am pleased with your performance!
- You're doing well at [tasks and responsibilities].
- Other people have told me [good things].
- Your hard work is very much appreciated.
- Your effort made a difference [in specific areas].

Kevin has invited Ivan to meet with him for a conversation about his performance. He begins,

> Ivan, I want you to know that we're pleased with how you've been doing. In your three years here, you have met expectations and handled multiple projects quite capably. Your colleagues tell me you are a great team player and are very reliable about getting things done on time, and we really appreciate that! You are a key part of the team—especially on that new customer forum we rolled out last quarter. Your graphics made it special!

Ivan smiles.

> Well, thanks! It's nice to know my work makes a difference. I enjoy collaborating with everyone, and it's always fun to see something I created out there on our website for people to see.

Challenge for Better Performance

After reinforcing the existing good behaviors of an average performer, it's time to challenge them to do more. Remember to build on the employee's existing performance levels and successes; frame the conversation in terms of what you want to see more of. If they have just received acknowledgment and validation for what they are already doing, they will be in a positive frame of mind to build on that and take it to the next level.

A simple communication key: Be sure not to say "but" when presenting the challenge. "But" tends to negate everything that came before it. A phrase like "You are doing well, but we want to see more" neutralizes the compliment. If you feel compelled to say "but," trying substituting "and."

- I believe you can improve on this performance, and I would like to see you succeed.
- You can build on your current performance and grow.
- I would like to see you do even better at [specific tasks or areas of responsibility].
- If you put in the effort, you can be rewarded with [specific rewards].
- What would motivate you to do even better?
- Where do you want to go from here?

Ivan and Kevin are having a conversation about Ivan's performance. He's been acknowledged and thanked for his contributions. Kevin is ready to challenge him to improve. He says,

Ivan, I think you can do even better! I want to see you grow in this role and be in line for bigger bonuses and a promotion. I'd also like to see you move into a leadership position among the designers.

Ivan seems surprised.

Wow, really? I'd like that!

Kevin says,

Great! You can build on what you do well and really take it to the next level. I particularly think you could help us with our training and skills workshops. I've noticed that you have a knack for explaining things to people so that they figure out the solutions to their issues quickly. People seem to go straight to you when they have a question!

Ivan grins,

Yeah, somehow I've become the go-to guy, especially with software questions.

Kevin nods.

That's true. Let me ask you: where do you want to go from here? What would motivate you to do even better?

Ivan thinks for a moment.

I like the bonuses and wouldn't mind more money. I'm particularly interested in the leadership role and a promotion, though. I feel like it's time to move forward in my career.

Kevin responds,

Great! I would like to see you start moving up. It would be great for you and this company.

With a few key questions, Kevin has a clearer picture of Ivan's future goals and motivation.

Soliciting Insights

To truly coach for better performance, take the time to solicit the insights of your employee. Workers will be much more engaged when it's a two-way conversation. Asking open-ended questions elicits their viewpoints and gets them invested in the processes and outcomes. Their own strengths and resources will be revealed and put into use.

- Where (else) do you see room for improvement?
- What can you do even better?
- What are you capable of?
- How can you build on your existing success?
- What opportunities do you see coming up where you can really shine?
- What do you need to do more of? What do you need to do less of?

   In soliciting insights from your employees, you might find out that they want to feel more engaged, or something has changed in how they work. In these cases, you would be well served to revisit Chapter 4, Know Your Employees, and explore the topics of employee engagement, working style, strengths, and wants and needs.

   Kevin asks Ivan,

I mentioned where I would like to see you improve, and I really want to know where you see opportunities for growth.

Ivan thinks for a moment.

I like the idea of getting more involved with training and skills development. I think we could do a lot more regular training for all the designers and artists so we're ahead of the curve instead of playing catch-up all the time.

(Notice that Ivan has taken a simple suggestion, training and skills, and pushed it to a level that benefits a whole group of employees—he's thinking beyond just himself and already showing leadership potential.)

Kevin responds,

> That sounds great! I think we can lay out a plan around that for sure. In terms of your current work responsibilities, what can you do more of to be even better?

Ivan says,

> Well, I started a priority to-do list when I get really busy, and that has helped me focus. If I did it every day, instead of just when I'm slammed, I would probably get more done.

Kevin says,

> Excellent idea! On the flip side, what do you need to do less of?

Ivan says,

> Oh, good question! I'd certainly like to spend less time in meetings and on conference calls. It not only takes up time, but can take me right out of my creative zone if I have to leave something unfinished to go to a meeting.

Then Kevin concludes with,

> Fair enough, we can talk about ways to minimize your time in meetings and on conference calls. I can see how that would distract from your flow.

In a short conversation, Ivan and Kevin have crafted some important insights. They continue to talk about this, and Ivan shows some surprisingly creative thinking. Kevin notes that maybe he should ask Ivan these questions more often.

Creating a Performance Plan and Accountability

After identifying areas for improvement and growth, it's time to get down to the nitty gritty and lay out an action plan. For this, you will use the techniques found in Chapter 6, Goal Setting, so review it for basic concepts and specific phrases and questions to use.

- How will you get from where you are now to where you want to be?
- Let's break this down into short-, medium-, and long-term goals.
- What are the first steps for you to take? Next steps?
- How can I support you in doing better? What do you need from me?
- How will you stay committed to this plan and your overall improvement?
- I know you can do this—go make it happen!

Kevin begins to help Ivan come up with a plan.

Ivan, these are great ideas, and I want to see you get the promotion you're looking for. How will you get there?

Ivan grins and says,

Well, first I want to ask if you can send me to the big images conference in three months. The vendor who makes all the graphics software and several other pieces of software we use hosts it once a year, and there are tons of workshops I can take to learn new techniques. I can come back and teach those techniques to the other designers.

(Ivan has asked for support, and already lays out the benefits of agreeing to send him to the conference.)

Kevin nods and makes a note,

That's a really good idea, and I'll see if I can make it happen. What else can you do?

Ivan thinks and says,

Well, I don't want to add to our meeting burden, but if I'm going to step up with training, then I want to have an occasional meeting or lock-up session where I can do some teaching.

He and Kevin talk about how to make this happen and schedule the first one to be a half-day meeting in two months. Ivan sets down some short-term goals of figuring out the training agenda, organizing some exercises, and other preparation. Then they have this conversation:

Kevin: As I said, I'm going to see about sending you to the images conference. How else can I support you as you improve?

Ivan: Check in with me about the training plan. I do well with a regular reminder—whether it's email or just dropping by my cubicle.

Kevin: Sure, I can do that. How often? Is once a week too much?

Ivan: That sounds good, since I want to get started right away. It'll keep me on task.

Kevin makes a note to check in with Ivan, then asks,

How will you stay committed to this plan?

Ivan grins,

That's a good question. Having events on the calendar with deadlines really helps me stay on track. I'm really excited right now, so maybe I should come up with a way to keep that excitement going!

Kevin: Good idea! How might you do that?

Ivan: Hmm. Well, I have this little ritual I do when I'm feeling time-crunched. I take a few minutes and listen to a particularly calming piece of music on my MP3 player and almost meditate, which helps me focus. I could do that with a more inspiring piece of music and think about what I'm trying to achieve. That might keep my energy up.

Kevin: That's really creative! I know you can do this, Ivan. You're going to go from good to great, and I can't wait to see how you get there!"

Ivan: Thanks, Kevin!

Kevin and Ivan close their conversation with a list of some short-term goals and next steps. Ivan is excited to get started on some of his new initiatives.

Chapter 13
Coaching Top Performers

Your top performers are your superstars. They consistently meet their lofty goals, objectives, and expectations and set a high level of productivity. You can rely on them to get the jobs done and done well. The challenge for coaching them is about keeping them happy, engaged, and continuing to perform at that level. You may have to offer more than just standard rewards with these performers, especially if they have been rewarded a lot already. You can think bigger and find lessons from your top performers that can be applied with other workers.

Before beginning to coach your top performers, ask yourself these questions:

- What do I know and what have I noticed about this employee?
- How can I keep this person performing at this level?
- How can I keep him motivated and engaged?
- How can this person be challenged to do even more?
- What do I know about how this person works that can be applied to other workers?

When you can answer these questions, you will be prepared to coach someone who is a superstar.

Joan is the owner of a large contemporary art gallery. There are six associates who work for her. They are variously responsible for coordinating exhibits by featured artists, event planning, publicity, care of the artwork, client relations, artist relations, and sales. Of the associates, Ramon is her top performer. He is efficient, creative, and has the highest sales in the gallery. Joan knows he has been approached by some other galleries to work for them. She really wants to keep him in her gallery and wants him to keep performing as well as he does. She asks herself what she knows about him, and this is what she comes up with:

- Ramon has strong interpersonal communication skills—he cultivates the relationships that bring new artists in and convince buyers to purchase.
- He presents creative suggestions and likes to take on new challenges. He created the gallery's social media presence and monthly newsletter, which have been very well received.
- He's already earned a raise and gets regular bonuses on his sales. He's expressed interest in accompanying Joan on trips to find new artists. He seems to have a good eye for what fits in with our gallery, as well as what will sell.

With these factors in mind, Joan has a conversation with Ramon one morning before the gallery opens.

Recognizing and Acknowledging High Performance

Letting your high performers know that they are appreciated is extremely important. People simply won't continue to give their all if it is not valued. Expressing your personal appreciation fosters a good relationship with your employees. Be specific in your praise!

- We really appreciate all your hard work.
- I am especially impressed with ... [specific achievements or characteristics].
- You really went above and beyond on [task or project]!
- Other people tell me ... [good things].
- Because of your work, we have been able to ... [describe positive results].
- Your contributions are noticed! You earned [something] in reward and recognition!

Joan smiles at Ramon and begins,

> Ramon, I want to take a few moments to thank you for all your hard work here at the gallery! You have the highest sales again this quarter, and I'm particularly impressed at the way you promoted our last opening reception! We had the highest turnout ever and sold three pieces right away!

Ramon smiles back,

> Well, thank you! I love putting together those opening receptions, it's so much fun. And I love making a sale, it's a bit of a thrill!

Joan agrees,

> I get that thrill, too. I'll have that commission bonus ready for you at the end of the month! I don't know if you know this, but your sales are really contributing to the growth I

had envisioned for this gallery. Because of your sales, we will be able to upgrade the computers this year and do some remodeling I've been wanting to do for ages! So thank you again!

He leans forward,

Wow, really? New computers will be awesome! What kind of renovations are we going to do?

(Note that Ramon asks what *we* are going to do. He's obviously an engaged and committed employee, a common trait of high performers.)

They discuss the renovations for a few minutes before moving on.

Reinforcing Desired Behaviors

If something works, do more of it. This is the attitude you want to reinforce in your employees. Be specific about what you want to continue seeing from them or seeing even more of. Top performers can model good practices, behaviors, and techniques that observant coworkers can pick up on. Eliciting their thoughts on their successes gives you a chance to acknowledge their accomplishments again.

- Here is what I notice that you do extremely well . . . [specifics]. Keep at it!

- When this project went into meltdown, you kept a cool head and got us back on track in record time.

- Your attention to detail really paid off when we [completed specific task].

- I'm impressed with how you . . . .

Joan decides to get specific with Ramon.

> I notice that you are particularly good at creating relationships with our artists and our buyers. They seem to ask for you specifically! Those skills are creating lasting benefits for all of us. Thank you!

Ramon smiles widely,

> I guess I'm a people person!

Joan says,

> Well, yes, that's true. But I think it goes beyond that. You've used online media to connect with artists and customers to build or establish those relationships in a way the rest of us haven't quite managed to do. I like how you use your tech savvy in those relationships. Keep it up!

Soliciting Insights for Top Performance

If you solicit insights from your top performers, you will open up a gold mine of valuable information. You will hopefully learn what motivates and invigorates your superstars. You might also find ways to keep them loyal and focused, as well as finding out how they want to grow and where they might go next. With the right kinds of questions, you can elicit information that can support all your other employees as well.

- What are you most proud of?
- What do you do to ensure your success?
- What do you think is key to your accomplishments?
- What do you enjoy doing the most?
- What can you do even better?
- Where do you see room for growth?
- What more are you capable of?
- How can you build on your existing success?
- What opportunities do you see coming up where you can really shine?
- What do you need to do more of? What do you need to do less of?
- How can we expand your success to others?
- What would motivate you to keep up your performance levels?
- How can we challenge you to grow?
- What do you see as your next steps here?

Joan realizes that to keep Ramon happy and performing well in the gallery, she needs to find out what he wants to do there. He already earns regular sales bonuses and got a promotion to "senior associate" a year ago. There isn't a lot more room for advancement in the gallery, so she wants to ask him what he sees as the next steps. She begins,

> Ramon, you're doing really well, and I want to help you keep doing that and make sure you're happy here. Tell me a little about what you see as the key to your success.

Ramon thinks for a moment and responds,

> Well, as I said, I'm a people person, so that helps. I've always wanted to work in the art world, so this position has been great—I feel like I get to explore my passion.

(Note Ramon's use of the word *passion*. Many high performers are passionate about their work, which are major factors in their performances.)

Joan smiles,

> Oh, we notice your passion for art—it's infectious! Our artists and customers really respond to that, you know. It creates a positive vibe. I would like to help you explore that passion even more. What would you like to be doing here?

Ramon leans forward excitedly.

> Well, I think I have told you before that I really want to come with you on some of your trips to New York! I'd like to meet with the artists and customers there and see what you do when you go there.

Joan says,

> Yes, I remember you've expressed interest in that. Let's talk about it! I've got a five-day trip coming up in three months. I think you could help me connect with new artists in a stronger way. What would you specifically do during that trip?

Ramon responds,

Well, I've been in contact with a few New York City artists online, and I could set up meetings with them in person. I also have had inquiries from potential buyers in New York, and I would love to show them portfolios of the work we can offer. These are people with a lot of money, and an in-person conversation can really cultivate a relationship with them. Plus, there is an exciting modern photography exhibit at the Guggenheim I want to see.

Ramon puts his interests in terms of what will be of value to Joan's gallery, and he closes with a personal interest. He and Joan hash out a few more details of what he could do during the trip and why it would be valuable. She sees that the cost of taking Ramon on the trip (extra airfare, hotel, dining) would be well offset by the results he could bring in. Joan then says,

Well, your thoughts on this trip sound great, and I think we can make it work. Beyond that, what do you want to be doing here? If you could determine your next step, what would it be?

Ramon thinks for a minute, then says, somewhat hesitantly,

I've been noodling around with an idea for a more developed artist program. I have read about some other, larger galleries and museums that have a lot of artist support services, and I think we could develop that here.

Ramon has expressed interest in a pet project, which can be an excellent way to keep high performers invested, engaged, and excited about their work. High performers may seek a creative challenge (above and beyond what they already do well), and working with them to develop pet projects can keep them loyal and performing well.

Joan is intrigued and says,

> Tell me more about that. What would you create?

Ramon responds, his energy picking up,

> I thought we could teach our artists how to promote their own work, particularly online, so they could be our marketing partners. I can easily teach them how to build a simple website, use social media, and send out e-newsletters to their fans. That way, they can be driving people to our gallery for purchasing and helping us promote events that involve them. We can all cross-promote each other. We could also support them with tutorials on mounting and framing and other techniques. I'd like to have an artist's gala once a year to express our appreciation and connect them with buyers. And eventually, maybe in a few years, I think we could sponsor an artists' retreat to give them time to work and perhaps throw in a creative challenge for them.

Ramon's ideas are very forward-thinking. He sees ways to improve the gallery's relationship with artists and drive business to the gallery. He is thinking to the future to create a solid program that will benefit not just the gallery but the artists as well. Joan is impressed:

> Wow, those are great ideas. Let's talk about how to get started!

In this conversation, Joan has found out what might motivate Ramon and keep him happy at the gallery. She notices that his goals would really benefit the business, and he seems quite excited about the new opportunities.

Creating a Performance Plan
and Accountability

Once you have affirmed the performance of your super-stars and gotten the important insights in where to go next, it's time to put the ideas into practice. Review Chapter 6, Goal Setting, for basic concepts and specific phrases and questions to use. Here are some additional things you can say to move forward.

- How will you get from where you are now to where you want to be?
- Let's break this down into short-, medium-, and long-term goals.
- What are the first steps for you to take? Next steps?
- Here is what I would like to see from you in the next few weeks . . .
- How can I support you? What do you need from me?
- How will you stay committed to this plan?
- I know you can do this, so let's get started!

Joan and Ramon have been talking about next steps for Ramon in his career at the gallery. He's outlined some things he would like to do, as well as an exciting pet project. Joan turns the conversation to next steps.

> Ramon, let's figure out how to make these things happen. I'll be making the travel arrangements for the New York trip in a few weeks. What do you need to do to make the most of the trip?

The following conversation occurs:

Ramon: I'll arrange and schedule some artist meetings. There are at least three I want to meet with, and possibly two more if I can make the connections. I'll also connect with the buyers and see if I can schedule meetings with them. That means I need to update our portfolio and prepare some presentations for them.

Joan: That sounds great. Can you get me a tentative schedule by the end of the month?

Ramon: I think so. I'll probably have the portfolio updated and the presentation key points ready just before we leave.

Joan: That sounds fine. I'll check in with you and see how it's going, probably weekly, and then daily before the trip. I may have some other tasks for you then.

Ramon: That's great! I know it's an investment to take me along, so I'm happy to help with whatever you need.

Joan: Thanks, I appreciate that! Now, about this artist program. I think it's a great idea, and I want to challenge you to really take ownership of it. So what would be the first steps?

Ramon: Well, we could start small and low-cost, of course. I think the online marketing tutorials would be great things to roll out. You know, we already do a great online newsletter, and I could start a newsletter just for artists very quickly and at no extra cost. I could start by putting tips and techniques in there, and then look into an in-person class or more written tutorials. The other associates have some great tips to share as well, so we could all contribute.

Joan: Well, I appreciate that it can be launched without a lot of extra cost! What would be a reasonable deadline for getting the first artist newsletter out?

Ramon: It would really only take me a day or two to create the new mailing list. I could probably get the first newsletter out within two or three weeks. I'll need to develop the content a bit and get input from the other associates.

Joan: Wow, that fast? That's terrific! How can I support you with that?

Ramon: I would want you to read over the newsletter before sending it—make sure it's appropriate, and add anything you want. A personal message from the gallery owner to the artists would be great!

Joan: Sure, I can write that. Sounds like fun!

Ramon: I'm so excited! We can also use the newsletter system to create a poll and find out what our artists would like to see from us, so then we can create a really great development program. Oooh, that gives me another idea! In addition to the newsletter, we can create an "artist-only" section of our website and have it be full of resources.

Joan: Would that be hard to do?

Ramon: Not at all, it's simple to add a page. Once we write materials for the newsletter, they can be expanded a bit and put online. It can even be a hidden page, and only our artists would have the link. We have plenty of storage space on our server, so there's really no additional cost to add this kind of page.

Joan: Sounds good. When could you do that?

Ramon: I'd like to say I could do it right away, but it's probably more realistic to launch a new page after the New York trip. That will give me time to develop the materials and fine-tune them and not be in a rush.

Joan: That's great. I'll check in with you about the first newsletter, and then about the web page after our trip.

Part Three

B eing a team player is an attractive asset in any employee. Everyone in an organization works together to achieve the group's goals, mission, and vision. Whether or not you have clearly defined teams, teamwork is essential in today's business world. Well-functioning teams create a true synergy—contributions that are more than just the sum of what the individuals can create. High-performing teams can bring out the best in their members and be very productive.

It's important to remember the key distinction between groups and teams. A *group* of people have characteristics in common (such as gardening clubs or parenting support groups), whereas a *team* has a shared goal or task and must work together to achieve it. The goal is what unites a team. As a leader, you will be expecting teamwork. Coaching teams with this expectation builds a foundation for success.

Coaching teams is similar to coaching individuals, with a few key differences. You can certainly coach members one on one, but working with the whole team gives you the opportunity to tap into the "group mind." When people think beyond just themselves, they can become creative in new, bigger ways.

They will see connections among themselves and what they do that boosts everyone.

This part of the book gives you tools for confidently coaching teams, whether they are project-based or a standing team. You may find coaching teams to be most effective if you are the leader by position or designation, but many of these tools can be used by team members who are not leaders.

The Phases of Team Creation

When coaching a team, it is helpful to determine what stage of team evolution it is in. There are four main stages of teams: forming, storming, norming, and performing (covered in the following chapters in more detail). Forming is the first stage, when the team is created. Storming is usually next—brainstorming on goals, procedures, tasks, next steps. Norming is the reality check: The team gets to work, sees what happens, and begins to make adjustments and changes as needed. Performing is when things are running smoothly, goals are being achieved, and the results are noticeable. Truly exceptional teams may move on to a fifth stage: transforming. In this stage, they create results that have even bigger impacts and possibly influence changes throughout the organization or even the industry.

Knowing the stage of the team will help you keep your expectations appropriate and find the right questions to ask. These stages aren't necessarily linear, one-way, or evenly spaced. A team might sail through forming and storming and spend a long time norming, to the point that it sends them back to storming to make major adjustments. A performing team might have to deal with a major change (such as losing some key members to layoffs or reorganization) that sends them back to norming (or storming, or even forming) for a while.

Coaching Teams

Teams can be created for a wide variety of purposes. Some are created for a single goal, such as rolling out a new product or creating a new marketing campaign, and they more or less dissolve after completion. "Standing" teams or committees might be created to have ongoing goals; these teams might be responsible for a broader range of defined tasks. One example of a standing team might be a whole department of a company, such as legal, communications, research and development, or human resources.

Chapter 14
Forming Teams

Teams have a greater chance of success if they are formed deliberately, thoughtfully, with intention and purpose. This gives all members a chance to be engaged and involved in creating the team, encouraging buy-in from the very beginning. The forming stage creates the foundation for performance and success. Coaching at this stage can lead to big dividends later when the team starts performing. If the team goes through major changes at any point (losing or adding members, changes in goals), it can be beneficial to revisit the questions used in this chapter to re-engage and reinvigorate employees—and sometimes reinvent the team entirely. This stage is when each individual's role, responsibilities, and expectations are clarified. The individual buy-in will enable total team alignment toward one purpose.

Defining the Purpose of the Team

Defining and communicating the purpose of forming the team and the goals expected of them lends clarity to all future endeavors. The purpose is the whole point of having or creating a team, and it must be clear and obvious. Teams are often deliberately formed with a direct purpose in mind; other times, people come together for other reasons and then realize they are working in a team. In either case, the purpose should be well known among team members and reiterated from time to time.

- The purpose for forming this team is . . . .
- Our goals are . . . [be very specific].
- Our mission is . . . .
- When we achieve these goals, the effect will be . . . .
- Here's how our work affects the organization . . . .
- This work is important because . . . .
- Our team contributes to this organization's overall vision by . . . .
- Each member of this team was chosen for areas of expertise/experience/responsibility in the organization.
- Each team member will be held accountable for [the rules of engagement for the team here].

These are all declarative statements you can make. You can turn them into questions that will elicit the creativity and insights of team members and open up more possibilities for achievement.

- Why do you think you were asked to be on this team?
- What do you see as the purpose of this team?
- What are we going to accomplish?

- Why are our goals important?
- What is our mission?
- What will happen once we achieve these goals?
- How do our achievements affect the company? The industry?
- What opportunities might open up for us?
- How will each of you hold yourselves accountable for delivering your results to this team?

Let's use an example to illustrate these concepts. At Adworkit, a large advertising firm, a new team is being created to focus on a specific industry: health care. This is a new client area for the firm, and the team consists of account managers, project managers, writers, graphic artists, and a few others. At the very first meeting of everyone involved, the team leader, Sidney, presents the objectives for the team as laid out by the executives and gets input from members:

> Folks, we are hereby kicking off Adworkit's new health care team! As you know, health care is a client base we haven't fully gone after before, and we have had inquiries and requests from organizations in that industry. The execs thought it would be wise if we created this team so that we could fully serve clients in that field and grow the company into new areas. This way, we'll be positioning ourselves for success, rather than just trying to keep up.

> So here are our goals: Adworkit wants to sign at least three health care clients in the next six months, and expand that to six by end of the year. We are looking for revenues of $2 to $5 million brought in from signing these clients. Given all the services we offer and new ones that we want to develop, we think this goal is within reach. The impact here would be huge! As you know, our company mission is

> about helping our clients communicate their value to their customers. This is particularly necessary in the health care field right now, so we will be making quite a difference for our clients.

Sidney pauses and looks at the expectant, enthusiastic faces around him. He smiles.

> Okay, I've told you in a nutshell what we are expected to accomplish. I'd like to hear from all of you now—what do you see as the purpose or goal of this team?

There's silence for a few minutes as they think, and then the suggestions start coming in.

> I think we're going to build a solid new customer base, and hopefully the whole company will expand because of it.

> We have the skills and creativity to create some cutting-edge campaigns. I really want us to win a Clio!

> I think we can do even better than $5 million in revenue. I bet we could do $10 million!

Although Adworkit's new health care team had a clear set of objectives, you may experience some undefined or unclear situations in which the only guidance you have received from your leadership is "Make this happen" or "Fix this." In these cases, the defining questions about the purpose of the team will create the critical conversation to bring team members together and clarify goals and desires.

Crafting the Team Charter

A charter lays out how the team will function—the rules of engagement. It includes guidelines for how decisions are made in the team (e.g., consensus, democracy, single decision maker), how communications are handled (e.g., via e-mail, written, conference calls), and of course the purpose, goals, and mission. These are the ground rules for functioning, which create a springboard for better work. A clear charter is a key element for high-performing teams. The charter should be well communicated and understood by all team members. Discussing how to make decisions and communicate at the very beginning helps clarify procedures, which reduces confusion and allows everyone to get on with their tasks. Later, as you define roles and responsibilities, these should be added to the charter as well.

- Decisions will be made by . . . (or, How will decisions be made?)
- How will we communicate with each other?
- How should we track our achievements?
- How often will we meet?
- Who is the leader, if there is one?
- What, if anything, needs to be kept confidential?
- Is there anything that should be off limits for discussion in our meetings, or can we bring up any topic we want?
- What can be shared with our stakeholders, and when?
- Will we need to consult with or inform other people of what we're doing? If so, how and when?

Often, teams capture these rules of engagement in writing and each member signs the charter to formally demonstrate his commitment. In the world of coaching, actually writing something down can create a more powerful buy-in and motivate people to hold themselves accountable for their commitments. Keeping things confidential, if necessary or desired, can help create a safe space for the team to work. Opening up the table for any kind of discussion ("no sacred cows") creates free space for employees to feel comfortable sharing ideas or discussing problems and issues if they come up.

Sidney is pleased with the excitement on the faces of most of Adworkit's new health care team. After taking notes on the goals and thoughts of the team members, he begins to lay out the ground rules:

> All right, folks, let's take care of some housekeeping details. We have our goals and objectives, and I'm also excited about what you brought up! Two key areas where we need immediately clarity are decision making and communication. These will help us all do our best! Obviously, you are each responsible for your own tasks and are encouraged to make decisions that you're confident about. If you're uncertain about something, talk to the people who might be most affected by the issue, and try to come to a consensus. If you can't come to an agreement, or an executive decision needs to be made, come to me. I encourage all of you to make your voices heard—I want your thoughts and opinions before I made a decision that affects you.

Heads nod, and people make notes. Sidney continues,

> Next, we need to decide how we will communicate. Obviously, we should have regular meetings, but how often?

A few people murmur. A project manager speaks up,

> I'm in a lot of meetings already, and I'd like to limit our face time to something reasonable. Also, I work from home

sometimes, and I'd appreciate the chance to call in, if possible, rather than attend live.

Sidney nods,

Absolutely, we can arrange for a speaker phone and a conference line. What would be a reasonable frequency for meetings?

An account manager speaks up,

Well, we don't have signed clients right now, so I suggest maybe once a month until we have some projects in hand. Then maybe every other week or every week if we need to.

There are a few nods and murmurs of agreement. Sidney and the team hammer down a plan for meetings. He goes on to ask,

How should we communicate with each other?

Several people simultaneously say, "E-mail!" then laugh a bit. The group decides to create group space in the intranet where they can store files they all need, update project timelines, look at each other's schedules, and send e-mails to the whole group when necessary. Sidney makes notes to create this intranet subsite and invites everyone to join.

The roles of the individuals in the group are fairly clear already and are based on their positions in the company. After more discussion, they realize they need to keep one of the senior vice presidents in the loop—the woman who championed the existence of this team, worked to have it created, and is focused on growing this client base. She's extremely busy, and they decide that Sidney will update her via e-mail and phone calls as she is available.

Sidney challenges all of them to think beyond themselves and support the team's goals.

Learning about Each Other

In the forming stage of teams, you will all be figuring out how you work together, who does what best, and how you interconnect to create your results. You'll fine-tune this process during the norming and performing stages (Chapter 16). In the early stages of team formation, you can create engagement and buy-in by eliciting insights from the team members about what they do well and what they are excited about doing. You can also affirm the strengths, abilities, and behaviors that you already know exist in the team.

- You were specifically chosen for this team because of . . .
- I know that you are skilled and capable, which is why you were asked to contribute.
- What does each of us bring to the team in terms of capabilities, experience, skills?
- What is this team capable of?
- What does the team as a whole offer to our organization?
- How might we leverage our strengths in this team?
- What excites you about what we're going to do?
- What can we accomplish if we all work together?
- What have we learned elsewhere that we can apply in this team?
- What kind of support do we need to be successful?
- Is there anything you individually hope to gain and learn by being on this team? How can we help you gain that experience?

These kinds of questions will help the individuals in the team learn about each other, brainstorm on how to work well, and create an awareness of abilities and strengths as well as opportunities for growth for each member. When team members can see connections among themselves as well as what the whole group can offer, they can make use of their abilities and strengths in powerful and rewarding ways.

At Adworkit, Sidney is turning the conversation to the strengths and capabilities of his team members. Some of his employees are fairly new and don't know the others as well, and of course, even though some have been on teams before, this is an entirely new team created for a specific purpose. He says,

> You were all picked to be on this team for specific reasons. Some of you have expressed interest in or have experience in the health care field. Others have shown us how creative they can be when working on projects in unfamiliar terrain. We think this team will create amazing results. Let me ask you: What do all of you see as your strengths?

They end up going around the room, with each person briefly answering.

> I enjoy a challenge, and this sounds like a good one.

> I have medical illustration experience, which I haven't gotten to use here yet, so I'm excited!

> I have connections at three different pharmaceutical companies.

> I used to work at a hospital, so medical terminology is familiar to me.

> Call me nuts, but I enjoy creating and tracking a project from the very beginning through to the end.

Sidney nods, taking notes. He asks,

> If we consider all of these individual skills and strengths, and we put them all together, what do you think this team is capable of?

There is silence for a moment, and then an account manager, says,

> I can already tell that this team will offer start-to-finish dedicated support for advertising in the health care market. We can be the total package for our clients.

Several people nod. A project manager pipes up,

> I agree. And I think that we can find all-new ways to get our advertising message out—things we have never done before. I find that exciting.

Sidney affirms these thoughts.

> I think you're right, and I like to see this excitement! It will give us momentum to move forward and start making things happen. There's a lot we can do! Before we get to figuring out next steps and assigning tasks, I want to find out where you think we need some support.

One of the copywriters speaks up.

> I know there are some specific legal regulations in the health care field, particularly in pharmaceuticals, about what you can and can't say in advertisements. Can we get some legal counsel to review these materials, or possibly some training on these rules?

Sidney writes that down.

> Very good point. We will have legal counsel reviewing our work as we start—we're in the process of finding someone appropriate. I'll see what I can arrange in terms of some training! What else?

A project manager speaks up,

> I notice that we don't have any administrative assistants in this meeting. Will any be assigned to us? I think we will need their support as we get rolling.

Sidney says,

> Agreed. We can get some support from some of the existing administrative assistants, and as we get moving and productive, we may need to hire a full-time one dedicated to our team.

There are nods of agreement from around the room.

In this brief conversation, Sidney has affirmed some individual strengths and skills, as well as opened up the team conversation to seeing interconnections. He's also invited comment on where the team needs support.

Defining Roles and Responsibilities

In a professional environment, the roles and responsibilities of team members may be mostly defined by their jobs. If everyone on the team holds a similar position (e.g., a team of lawyers on a class-action suit), or if the goals or purposes go beyond regular job duties (e.g., a group working on employee morale), then getting input and commitment on roles and responsibilities can be extremely helpful. You might find that employees bring even more to the table than you thought; you might notice areas where you need some support. Well-defined roles and responsibilities bring clarity. Getting input from team members on roles will allow them to grow professionally, perhaps reaching a bit beyond what they have done before.

- What role does each team member play?
- Who will do what?
- What is each person responsible for?
- How else can you support this team?
- How will we work together?
- How does the work flow through our team?
- Should we change any existing procedures and, if so, how?
- What is and is not within the scope of our responsibility as a team?
- Let's role-play some examples and see where we believe our roles would come into play.

Revisiting roles and responsibilities at various points after team formation will shed light on how changes have affected the team and the individual members. You'll be able to see what's working well and what needs adjustment.

Sidney begins to wrap up the health care team kickoff meeting at Adworkit. He has helped his team learn about each other, and now he wants to clarify roles and responsibilities. He says,

> I want everyone to be clear about what each of us does on this team, so let's go through it the way the client would encounter it. Let's say that we get a major hospital as a client—the contract is signed! What happens then?

One of the account managers pipes up,

> Well, whichever account exec worked with the EVP on getting this client would take over the major communications. We take the contract deliverables and call up our project managers to decide who heads up each project. We're responsible for maintaining contact with the clients to update them on what we're doing and also communicating with everyone else on any changes or notes from the client.

Sidney nods,

> Good! And project managers, what do you do?

One of them says,

> We look at the deliverability and the timelines, and figure out the benchmarks, the resources, the tasks, and the people involved to make it happen. We assign work to our writers, graphic artists, layout, and other specialists to start creating the materials. We determine if we need to send work out to contractors and whom to choose. We keep track of who is doing what and when, we communicate with the account managers, and we make sure our team members have the resources they need to do the work on time and on budget.

Sidney smiles,

> Excellent! What's next?

A writer speaks up,

Well, the whole creative team gets to work simultaneously. The writers start work on their copies, which are usually reviewed by the head writer, the account manager, and sometimes legal. The graphic designers start creating the look of the product, with input from the client via the account manager. If we are working with contractors, we make sure that we are communicating with them and they get what they need from us. We have several rounds of revisions, usually, after input and review from the clients.

Sidney says,

Sounds effective! Terrific, it seems like you all know what you'll be doing, since it's more or less how things flow around here. How might we do things differently?

It's an unexpected question, and it stumps the team for a minute. Then a project manager speaks up.

I would suggest that it might be helpful to have project managers sit in on the early meetings with clients. We hardly ever have direct contact with clients, and it would help us create a smoother process if we could answer questions they have and be very clear on what they want so we can deliver it.

Sidney says,

Excellent suggestion! Let me see if we can make that happen. Anybody else?

A writer says,

I'd love to see us hire an editor, or promote one of the writers to editor. The writers all tend to review each other's work, but it can be hard to fit that in with all our responsibilities. I think having a dedicated editor, especially one with experience in health care, would be really useful—we can deliver a better final product and probably faster, too.

Several other creative team members are nodding in agreement.

Sidney writes down the editor suggestion. He decides to wrap up the kickoff meeting with some words of support and encouragement before dismissing the team.

Chapter 15
Brainstorming

The second major phase of team formation is storming, or brainstorming. This is when the team creates the new ideas for how they will achieve their goals or fulfill their purposes. Brainstorming can happen around any particular task or problem to solve. It can be a powerful tool for creating even bigger ideas for a team to embrace. Done just after team formation, it sets the tone for everything that follows. Brainstorming can, of course, be done at any later point as well, especially if changes are necessary. The storming phase can also be the team's launch into action.

Setting a tone of trust and safety for the team will allow them to open up during brainstorming. If you've taken the time to get to know your team and lay down the ground rules for how you function, team members will feel confident bringing their innovative ideas forward.

Tapping the Group Mind

One of the major benefits of a team is that it can create true synergy—something greater than the sum of its parts. Brainstorming with a team will open up more possibilities because people will be thinking beyond just themselves and will respond to other suggestions with new creativity. Set the tone for group brainstorming by helping the individual people start to think as a team. Notice that you'll be stressing the plural pronouns: *we* and *us.*

- As we start to brainstorm, I encourage you to think beyond yourselves.

- Think about us, and not just you.

- Broaden your perspective as we create new ideas to achieve our results.

- Allow the team's energy to infuse your thinking as we brainstorm.

- Listen to each other, and let your teammates' words inspire you.

In this chapter, we'll use a running example to illustrate the storming stage of team formation. Desmond is leading a meeting of the new charity action team at his workplace, a large engineering firm. The team has six members and they come from all levels and departments of the organization. They are responsible for some charitable donations and involvement by the company as well as coordinating charity efforts on site, like blood drives and fundraisers. Their goals are to give a total of $100,000 to charitable groups (some corporate funds, some raised from employees) and get at least 30 percent of the company's workforce involved in some way (donations, volunteering).

Desmond kicks off the meeting by challenging the team members to brainstorm.

Welcome to the Charity Team brainstorming meeting! I think we're all excited about what we'll do this year. We will start sharing ideas shortly, but first I want to challenge all of you to think bigger. Share your thoughts and ideas, and really listen to each other. We can all build on ideas together to create something really special. Let's trust each other and grow together!

Generating Ideas

Obviously, the whole point of brainstorming is to generate new ideas. To keep a creative flow, establish the ground rules for initial brainstorming. All ideas should be considered or written down—even the half-joking ones that defy the laws of physics and time. You'll sort through ideas later (see the next section, Sorting Ideas and Reality Checks). By keeping the ideas open and not rejecting them, you'll keep the gates to creativity wide open. Be clear when you lay out the ground rules.

- All ideas are welcome!

- If it occurs to you, please share it—we really do want to hear it. We'll sort through the ideas later.

- We're just spitballing ideas right now; we will get to implementation and realistic concerns later.

- There is no judgment on the ideas, we are just gathering them right now.

- Let's stay in the "what if."

- When we put our heads together, we can really do some innovative thinking.

- Let's focus on possibilities and opportunities, rather than on things we can't do.

- Keep all of your comments constructive and positive.

After you have challenged your team members and laid the ground rules (including who will record the ideas), you can move on to powerful questions to spark the conversation.

- How might we accomplish our goals?

- What else can we do?

- How could we think about this differently?
- What have we done before that worked?
- What have other teams with similar goals done in these situations?
- What would an outside person have to say?

Be sure to validate everyone's ideas—find ways to thank them or at least acknowledge their efforts.

Desmond continues the Charity Team meeting by opening the floor for brainstorming. He says,

> Okay folks, we are going to start putting our ideas out there. At this stage, let us know your ideas—all of them, even the ones that sound crazy! I'll write them down. We will sort them later and decide what's realistic and what's not, so don't worry about that yet. There's no judgment in this space. Let's put our minds to work together!

There are smiles and nods around the room. He continues,

> You know our goals—$100,000 in charitable contributions and 30 percent workforce involvement. How will we do it?

It seems everyone has something to say at once, so Desmond decides to go around the room one at a time to start with.

> Last year, our blood drive was really popular, and I know the Red Cross would like to come back. I think we could publicize it even more and open it up to other companies in this area. [Something that worked in the past, planning to make it even better.]

> My friend at Giant Computers said that her company will match employees' charity donations. I wish we did that here! Maybe we could talk to the execs about that. [Reaching for a big change on a company level, learning from what someone outside the organization experiences.]

One of the local high schools runs a huge food drive every year. I want us to partner with them and help make it even better.

I help lead a Girl Scout troop, and I would love to see this company get involved, especially in teaching young girls about career opportunities in engineering. Not everything the Charity Team does has to be about money. [Creative suggestion that goes beyond just raising money; personal investment.]

The brainstorming continues, with people coming up with some dynamic ideas. They know they won't all be implemented, but they seem to enjoy sharing their thoughts.

Sorting Ideas and Reality Checks

Only *after* the brainstorming is complete should the ideas be sorted and decided on. Usually, not everything can be implemented from the brainstorming session. Raw creativity and big ideas can be made reality with judicious thinking about what is realistic and relevant, plus other concerns.

Before rejecting ideas, think about asking questions to learn more. Even if you have seen a particular idea fail in the past, listen carefully to see if the timing may be right now.

- What idea are we most excited about?
- What might have the best chance for success?
- Where should we focus our efforts?
- What's realistic for us?
- What considerations do we need to take account of?
- What haven't we thought of yet that might have an effect?
- Realistically, what can we do?
- What makes sense for us?
- Who will be affected by this? What might they have to say about how we do it?
- Who are the other stakeholders? What might they have to say?
- If we succeed in this, what else might happen?
- If we fail, what might happen then?
- What do we need to make this happen?
- Has anyone else done this before? What did they do that worked? What didn't work?

Bringing these questions to bear on the raw ideas from

brainstorming will help shape them into an actionable plan. It will also reveal who has done research or background work on implementing their ideas. Review Chapter 6, Goal Setting and let it guide you on turning goals and ideas into successful reality.

Desmond's Charity Team has come up with some really creative ideas for reaching their objectives. They take a 10-minute break before returning to start sorting through the ideas. (Desmond wanted them to have a mental "clear the slate" moment before coming back to reality.) They come back with fresh coffee, ready to get down to brass tacks.

> All right folks, we've got a terrific variety of ideas. Let's start figuring out what we're going to actually do. What are we most excited about?

A colleague speaks up,

> I am really intrigued by the matching donations idea. I would love it if my contributions were doubled, and I know lots of other people who would like that, too. I admit it seems like a long shot, but how could we get that to happen?

The person who originally suggested matching donations says,

> I did a little research on how matching donation programs work and talked to a friend of mine who works at a non-profit. I think I could put together a proposal for the executives to review, if all of you would help me.

There are several offers of support. Desmond says,

> Think about what we know about this company and our executives. What do we need to consider if we're going to put this proposal forward?

One person responds,

> Well, they have increased our charitable giving budget, so they clearly want to give more. Even so, I think we will have to put together some compelling reasons for them to approve a matching donations program. They like to see data, so I'll find some surveys on companies that have such a program.

Someone else adds,

> I love the idea, but I think that we shouldn't count on such a program being implemented right away. Even if they agree to it, it would probably be at least a year before it's rolled out. We can set it up to happen later, but I don't think we should count on it as a way to reach our $100,000 target.

Desmond makes notes about all these thoughts and how they might impact the matching donation proposal. In this conversation, the team has shown excellent insights when taking an idea and bringing it into the real world by considering the realities of pitching and creating such a program. They continue to sort through the rest of the ideas, figuring out what is doable and to what extent.

Assigning Tasks to Team Members

Once a team has brainstormed and then selected ideas for implementation, you'll pull in the techniques covered in Chapter 6, Goal Setting. Break down each goal and idea into a timeline of realistic tasks and procedures. Then the team will be able to get to work with their assignments. With an engaged and energetic team, you may have volunteers ready to get to work immediately, committing to tasks as they are being created. Sometimes, assignments will be obvious based on job duties. In other cases, you may need to ask who will do what, which can be an opportunity to find out what your team members are capable of and interested in. (You can also review Chapter 7, Meetings, for tips on defining roles in and responsibilities of the team.)

- Who will commit to these action steps?
- Who will take responsibility for and ownership of this task/procedure?
- What's coming up that we need to account for?
- How will we support each other in our tasks?
- How will we stay committed to our next steps?
- How can we all contribute?
- What will we celebrate at our next meeting?
- Let's put our enthusiasm to work and get going!

The questions here and the last statement are intended to help launch the team into action. When it's time to move from ideas to tasks, you can use the enthusiasm and energy from brainstorming and allow that positive energy to motivate the team to getting started strongly.

The Charity Team meeting has crafted some great

ideas with their brainstorming session, and then they hammered out some specific goals and first steps to take. Desmond starts to wrap up the meeting with assignments and commitments. Since this team isn't defined by job duties, they sort the work out according to abilities and commitments.

Desmond says,

Okay, we need to get to work so we can get some momentum going. In terms of the proposal for the execs to consider the matching donations program, who will do the research we talked about?

Pam, the project manager who suggested the matching donations program, says,

I will do the research, but I'd like some help writing the proposal, since I haven't done that before, and my work slate is pretty full. Can someone help me out?

The publicity/PR employee on the team offers to help, since she has experience with proposals and knowledge of the executives in the company. A couple of other people offer to help connect Pam with resources for her research.

Desmond writes this down. He says,

Pam, matching donations was your suggestion, and I'm delighted that you're starting the research. Can we count on you to lead this project and take responsibility for the timeline?

Pam nods.

Yes! I think it's a great idea, and even if it doesn't go into effect for a while, I really want to make it happen. So, everyone, I might come to you now and then for help with the next steps!

Desmond smiles,

Of course, we are a team, after all! Let me ask you this: How will you make sure you stay committed to this project throughout the year?

Pam thinks a moment.

Well, I'm pretty fired up about it, but I know it's sometimes hard to keep up that enthusiasm. I'll get started right away so I can get some momentum going. If I get the ball rolling and see the progress, that will help me stay on track. But I also will do well if people check in with me and ask how it's going.

Desmond nods and says,

Well, we will have monthly meetings, and we'll ask for your status updates. Let's all make a point of asking Pam how it's going and offering our support, okay?

There are nods and smiles around the room. The team works on assigning other roles, action steps, and responsibilities for the various tasks they brainstormed and shaped.

The meeting draws to a close, and Desmond says,

Folks, this was a great start to the Charity Team work for this year. I'm excited and pleased about the direction we're taking. We can make it happen, and I believe we will exceed our goals! Let's get to work!

Chapter 16

Norming and Performing

After forming and storming, teams will spend the bulk of their time norming and performing. These two stages are somewhat fluid and often overlap. Getting to work after brainstorming involves testing the waters, seeing what works and what doesn't, which is known as norming. There may be a learning curve if team members need to train on new techniques or procedures. Changes, disruptions, and opportunities can take a well-performing team and send them back to make adjustments before starting to perform again. The techniques and phrases offered in this chapter will probably be used over and over again in the life of a team.

Making Progress and Getting Momentum

As the team is getting to work after brainstorming, there may be a steep learning curve, especially if you are trying new things or team members are stretching beyond their comfort zones. Even if tasks are familiar and well known, working with a team may be new to everyone involved, so there will be functional learning in that respect. Interpersonal dynamics will come into play, and it may take a while to work the kinks out and get to a smooth performance. After getting to work, you'll probably have a check-in meeting of some kind (probably several, and likely regular status meetings as well).

- How is it going?
- What have we done so far?
- Have we reached the milestones we wanted to reach at this time?
- What's coming up next?
- What's working? What isn't?
- How are we interacting with each other?
- How is the team dynamic affecting us? Where do we need to make adjustments?

At a biological research facility of a large university, a Safety Team has been formed of the office manager, the facilities supervisor, one of the professors, a postdoctoral associate, and a few lab techs. Their founding goals were not just to reduce accidents but to take a much more proactive approach to safety and awareness. The team brainstormed for a while and started work on creating some safety training for all employees (especially the undergraduate work-study students), researching new kinds of safety inspections and certifications, and finding out about best practices of safety in research labs. They meet to discuss the past three months of their progress and upcoming milestones.

Christina, the office manager, is the team leader. She begins by saying,

> We've all kept up to date on our activities via e-mail, which I appreciate! Let's check in with each other now. How's it going with our first steps? What have we managed to get done?

They go around the room. The postdoc says,

> I went to a conference last month and really enjoyed the sessions on new best practices in lab safety. I learned a lot about what we could do, and maybe some loftier goals we can reach for in the future.

The facilities manager says,

> I am looking into the more advanced safety inspections and certifications. I'm waiting on some more information. It turns out there are a lot of options available to us.

A lab tech, Ron, says,

> I've been informally polling some of the undergrads about safety, to find out what they already know and what they need to know. I've heard some interesting things, but it's slow going. I had planned on having a proposal ready for some training and other changes, but I ran out of time to put one together.

Another lab tech chimes in,

> I've done the safety walkthrough of my area, as you all suggested, and found it really interesting. I had no idea safety officers had to look at so much stuff!

Christina smiles.

Yes, it's eye-opening, isn't it? It sounds like we're all mostly on track. Ron, we can help you with the employee polling and proposal. Let's talk about our next milestones.

The group discusses next steps and their goals for the next quarter, figuring out action steps and committing to them as they go. They brainstorm a bit on helping Ron get his proposal together in the next two weeks. Christina turns the topic to the team dynamic.

Folks, how is the e-mail working for you? It's great for me to keep track of who's doing what, but how is it working for the rest of you?

The professor says,

Frankly, it's a little difficult for me to do frequent updates via e-mail. I'm either teaching, conducting research, holding office hours, or in meetings. I don't get a lot of time to compose e-mail. I do read what you all send, but if you don't hear much from me, it's because I just don't have a lot of time.

Christina asks,

What can we do about that?

The group brainstorms a bit, and the postdoc offers to get updates from the professor verbally and include those in her own e-mails.

Facing Opportunities and Challenges

Changes will come along that inevitably affect a team. These may range from the small to the very large. Changes that might impact a team include members taking medical or family leave (or leaving the organization altogether), layoffs, budget reductions, changes in team goals, even severe weather or power outages. For problem solving, carefully review Chapter 9, Problem Solving, and use appropriate techniques and phrases that appear there.

Not all changes have to be negative. Good changes might mean more people hired for your team, an increased budget, or new technology that supports your work. These are opportunities in which the team can excel.

- What can we foresee happening that might affect us?

- What are our challenges?

- How do we address those challenges?

- How will we learn and grow from those challenges?

- What didn't go according to plan, and what are the effects of that?

- Did anything good happen in the midst of the challenge? How can we capitalize on that?

- How will we get back on track? Do we need to make an entirely new plan?

- What went better than expected, and what are the effects of that?

- Where are our opportunities? How can we take advantage of them?

- How does this new opportunity open up new possibilities for us?

In one of the Safety Team meetings, the team is discussing how their projects have been going. There has been some safety training for undergrad students in the lab and an immunization event for everyone working with live animals. A thorough safety inspection of all the mechanical and electronic lab equipment was conducted and turned up only a few minor repairs to be made. A fire drill showed that most people knew the evacuation routes and procedures. However, a month ago, a machine in one of the labs had a major breakdown during the night, spilling a great volume of a slightly hazardous chemical, which caused a flood on that floor that leaked down two more floors, creating a lot of damage. The emergency is over, the chemical is safely cleaned, and plans are being made for the renovations that will be necessary. The team is discussing what they learned from the event.

Christina asks,

Folks, I have to say I am impressed at how well we and the department as a whole handled the chemical flood last month. Obviously, we still have a lot of repairs to make. This was a big challenge! What did we learn from it?

The facilities manager speaks up,

Well, I'm proud that we had no injuries or illnesses because of it, and we were quickly able to locate the manual for the machine and the material data safety sheets for the fluids. Thanks to our procedures, we knew just who to call to come help us with the mess, and we were able to clean it up pretty fast. You hope you never have to test some of these disaster procedures, but it's confirming to know that they work!

The professor pipes up,

I was impressed by the immediacy of the communication

to everyone who works here. I knew we had a procedure in place in case of a disaster like this, but to see it at work firsthand was reassuring. My lab and I all got text messages, and the other professors did, too—so it was helpful to know we couldn't come in right away. I appreciated the regular updates and how you worked with us to let us attend to our lab animals or experiments that needed supervision.

A postdoc says,

I think I see an area for improvement. We found the manual for the machine right away, true, but we couldn't find the warranty information for quite a while afterward. That was an expensive piece of equipment, and it's crucial to have it up and running, or repaired, without ruining our operating budget or draining our grant money. I think we should have an organizing project for all the labs to have manuals, safety data sheets, and warranty and repair information in a central location.

There are nods of agreement and murmurs of "good idea!" Christina writes the suggestion down and they explore the idea a bit more.

After a while, Christina asks,

Okay, folks, looking forward, what opportunities are available to us?

There's a brief silence as they think. The facilities manager then says,

Well, we will have to do some major renovations to the building because of the chemical flood. That might be a good chance to install some updated safety equipment, like more convenient eyewash stations. We'll also have the opportunity to do a major review and inspection of the ventilation, electrical, and plumbing systems, since the walls will be down for a while.

A postdoc speaks up,

> I just got an invitation to a lab safety one-day conference in Massachusetts that I think would be beneficial! There will be some speakers and workshops, plus of course vendors and product showcases. I'd like to attend and see what kind of information or fresh ideas we could use.

A lab tech volunteers to go, too. Christina notes she will have to check the departmental budget for funds to send them.

In this conversation, the Safety Team has drawn lessons from a catastrophic event and identified opportunities for growth and learning.

Course Adjustment for Teamwork

For all teams, there will need to be course correction from time to time. People aren't machines to be set in motion, who will continue to work perfectly forever. Regular check-ins or status meetings can help all be aware of where and how things need to change. Tapping into the group mind and team thinking can help changes flow smoothly and engage the team members in what's going on. If major changes come along, you can use the tools in the previous section, Facing Opportunities and Challenges. Bring in the phrases here any time to assess how things are going and where some changes might be appropriate and wise.

- What's working? What's not?
- What do we need to keep doing?
- What do we need to do differently?
- What can we do even better?
- Are we meeting our milestone goals?
- If we're behind, how will we catch up?
- If we're ahead of schedule, how might we use this momentum to do more?
- How will we meet our next set of goals and obligations?
- What else do we need to be aware of?
- What do we need to prepare for?

The Safety Team at the university biological research department is holding a meeting in late April, toward the end of a busy academic year. There have been no major safety events in the past few months, renovations from the chemical flood are going well, and their other projects are proceeding apace. After some chitchat and general updating, Christina says,

> All right, team, let's think over the past six months and to what's coming up. What's working for us?

There's a chorus of positive statements about the team's improved communications, the renovations, and the ideas brought back from the safety conference. The group is particularly proud of the continued safety training efforts and how well they have worked. Attendance has been good, and there have been notably fewer injuries and accidents in the labs.

Christina asks,

> Is anything not working? Do we need to do anything differently?

A postdoc speaks up,

> I think our reporting system is a little too difficult for people to use. I know that one graduate student got a mild burn in the lab—nothing serious, but she didn't know she needed to fill out the safety incident form until weeks later when I asked her about it. When she did finally do it, she said it was really confusing. I think we can make it easier to navigate and fill out.

The group brainstorms around this issue for a while. Christina asks,

> What else do we need to be aware of?

The professor says,

> Well, I'm going to be taking a visiting professorship in Georgia next academic year, so I won't be here much. You will need to find another person to fill my spot on the team.

Christina asks,

> Okay, good to know. What else is coming up that we need to prepare for?

The facilities manager says,

> I just got notice that we'll have a safety audit by the university's OSHA office in a few months. I'll have to work on getting our data on accidents and injuries, plus the full report of the chemical flood and our safety inspections. We have a while to prepare, and we can use the time with the auditors to get guidance on more proactive steps we can take.

The team discusses how to prepare for the audit. A lab tech says,

> Thinking ahead to the next academic year, we will of course have a new influx of graduate students and undergrads in a few months. We should plan for an orientation safety workshop. We'll have the summer to work on it.

With this conversation, the Safety Team has figured out what's working and should be continued, what needs some attention and changes, and preparation for upcoming challenges and opportunities.

Chapter 17
Team Success and Achievement

A well-functioning team will create success by achieving at least some of its goals. A high-performing team can achieve all of their goals and sometimes much more. It's important to acknowledge success and celebrate achievement in the team framework. Doing so keeps individual members engaged, adds momentum to the team's work, and honors the value the team created. Successes should be acknowledged and celebrated at each milestone, as well as at final goal achievements (if there are any). Coaching questions can help the team members keep performing well to build on each success and look for deeper meaning in their achievements.

Acknowledging Success

Just like individual employees, the team as a whole should get a pat on the back now and then. Acknowledging accomplishments and achievements helps members stay happy, committed, and engaged. You definitely want to notice and reward positive behaviors so that you'll see more of them. Celebrate all the milestones! Encouragement and acknowledgment at each phase can inject new energy into a long project.

Remember to be timely and very specific in what you praise and acknowledge. In a team setting, you can and should acknowledge individual achievements, celebrating them with the whole team. Don't stop there—be sure to draw attention to the achievements of the team, how well everyone worked together, the successes of the group as a whole.

For acknowledging individual contributions, you can use the following phrases. Remember to be specific in your praise.

- Your work on [goal, milestone, project] was outstanding.

- We particularly liked how you . . . [specific action or accomplishment].

- Your work significantly impacted the team's accomplishments.

- You have been a crucial member of this team, and your contribution is very much appreciated.

- I've noticed that you seem motivated and energetic, and it brings up the energy of the rest of the team. Your positivity is really felt.

- To what do you attribute your success so far? Would you share that with the team to help us create best practices?

- How has working within this team helped you do your best? How have you helped others do their best?

In a group meeting, you can solicit opinions and acknowledgment from the rest of the team about individual performance as well.

- Who is proud of what they've done? Tell us about it!
- How has the success of an individual member affected the rest of the team?
- Who has been an unsung hero, and why?
- Who else should we be acknowledging and celebrating?
- Who has stepped up their game on this team?
- How have we made each other better?
- How has our work together created the team outcome?

Add specific comments on what you have noticed, such as,

I was impressed at how Marvin handled the communication with the unhappy client. That could have been a real mess and some of us were panicking! But he smoothed the situation calmly, found out what they really wanted, and led us into creating a great solution. Thanks, Marvin!

For celebrating team success and achievements, you can say the following.

- We did it! We accomplished . . . [specific achievements].
- We are tracking well toward our ultimate goal! We have reached the following milestones . . . .
- I'm impressed at how we . . . [give specific feedback].
- Our work really made a difference! [give specific examples of how].
- Think back to when we first formed as a team. How far have we come?

- What else are we proud of? What else have we done that deserves celebrating?
- What are the effects of our success? What's happening because of what we achieved?

Reviewing Challenges for Key Learnings

With regular status meetings and updates, a team will have been reviewing challenges, opportunities, and learnings along the way. It may be wise to have a thorough review (say, once or twice a year) about key learnings and challenges so that the team can celebrate their successes and figure out how their work can be applied elsewhere in the organization. If the team has a time-limited existence (for instance, a strategic planning team that is meant to exist for only two years), a major review of learnings, challenges, and opportunities would be appropriate as they close their activities and write reports. Some teams have rotating members (i.e., each member serves a specific term and then new members come in), who conduct a thorough review and communicate key learnings to the new team. Sometimes, the rest of the organization would benefit from knowing about the team's activities, so a clear delineation of challenges, learnings, and opportunities can benefit the other employees.

In any case, a team meeting that discusses challenges in the past will be looking back on a period of time and seeking insights. Tap into the team mind for powerful knowledge.

- What did we foresee happening? What actually happened?
- What were our challenges?
- How did we address those challenges?
- How did we learn and grow?
- What didn't go according to plan, and what were the effects of that?

- [Task or goal] didn't go forward as we hoped. How did that happen?
- Did anything good happen in the midst of challenges? How did we capitalize on that?
- How can we [team or organization] prevent mistakes from happening in the future?
- How did we get back on track from disruptions?
- What did go according to plan, and what were the effects of that?
- What went even better than expected, and what were the effects of that?
- What did we learn from how we worked and created our outcomes?
- What were the key learnings from our challenges and our successes?
- What might be challenging in the future?
- If we reflect back on this situation, what did we learn about ourselves individually and as a team?
- What surprised us (good and bad)?
- What did we learn that the rest of the organization can benefit from?
- How did our work impact the rest of the company (or industry)?
- Who else is affected by what we've accomplished?

Identifying New Opportunities

Once a team has achieved its milestones and primary goals, there may well be new opportunities ahead. A team that continues to exist will keep on working—say a group of trainers who focus on training others on a single software product. It is wise to seek and identify new opportunities to keep members engaged and to offer chances for growth. Doing the same old thing over and over is mentally tiring for a lot of people, who will disengage and "check out" from what they are doing. By looking for new opportunities, the team can create even more exciting solutions, stay committed and involved, and possibly move from performing to transforming.

- What has our work opened up for us, both as individuals and as a group?
- What new opportunities (and challenges) lie ahead for this team?
- What else could we do?
- How can we take what we've done and make it even better?
- How can we bring even more value to our organization?
- Where are the opportunities within this team? Within this company? Within this industry?

Determining Next Steps

A time-limited team (e.g., a review committee that is tasked with studying a certain subject and generating a policy report) will be disbanding after achieving their goals. At the completion of work, it's good to have a conclusion meeting and a warm send-off. You'll obviously be acknowledging and celebrating achievements, and you can then create a bridge to what's next for the team members.

- As we finish our tasks and celebrate our results, what do we see is the impact of our work?
- What might happen because of what we've done?
- What is next for each of us? For all of us?
- What did you learn or do here that will affect how you work in the future?
- What did the experience of working in this team mean for you?

A team with rotating members (i.e., a professional organization chapter, which will have new officers every year), changing members (incoming and outgoing, perhaps due to layoffs or new hires), or another set of goals to achieve will continue to function, possibly in new ways. A review meeting will lay the groundwork for the next steps—whether that is incorporating new members, changing responsibilities after losing members, or gearing up for new goals and achievements.

- What is ahead for this team as a whole?
- How do we prepare incoming and new team members? What do they need to know? How can we set them up for success?

- What legacy are we leaving to the new team?
- How do we smooth the transition for the new team members? How do we keep the momentum going for them?
- How do we build on our existing successes and achieve the next level of goals?
- What lessons from our first round of achievements can be applied to our next set of goals?

After major changes (e.g., new members, new goals), the team may well head back to the earlier stages of norming, storming, or even forming, so review the phrases in those appropriate chapters as needed. Remember, these stages are fluid, and revisiting them when needed will help build stronger teams.

Part Four

Perfect Phrases for Using Coaching Techniques with Superiors

Your superiors, upper management, founders, and top leaders drive the organization to achieve their mission and make their vision a reality. They are the decision makers. You probably function as a liaison between them and the frontline employees you coach. Most likely, you won't be directly coaching people above you in the hierarchy (many executives have their own professional coaches). However, you can use coaching-style questions and communication to find out what they really want, how they want it done, how they envision your role and that of your employees, and more. Smart leaders should come to you from time to time to ask about what's happening among your employees, and hopefully they will ask some of the same questions you find here.

The chapters in this section offer you phrases to support communication, relationship building, and navigating change initiatives. You'll be using these phrases mostly for your own elucidation and for helping your employees. However, they will also inspire your leaders to think bigger and communicate with you on new levels. All of these benefits can come together to keep an entire organization performing well.

Chapter 18
Communication

E xcellent communication within an organization can turn a good company into a great one. Engaged employees like to know what is going on and appreciate it if they feel heard and respected. Workers appreciate honest, direct communication from their leadership, especially in uncertain times. You can demonstrate solid communication techniques when speaking with those above you in the company. Asking coaching-style questions opens the door to important ideas and thoughts that you can, in turn, communicate to your employees. Consider your leaders as valuable resources, which you can tap into for your benefit and for the betterment of those you lead.

Eliciting Visions of the Big Picture

Upper management in a company is concerned with delivering on the organization's mission, creating value for all stakeholders, and achieving the vision of the company. As a manager, you are in a unique position to work with employees to engage and connect with the vision and mission, and by communicating well with your leaders, you can feed that engagement back up the ladder. Use the following phrases with upper management to gain clarity for yourself and to elicit information to share with those you coach and work with.

- How do you interpret our mission and vision?
- What do you expect us to accomplish and how?
- What excites you about our work here?
- How do we fit in within our industry? How do we stand out?
- What do you want for this company? What do you want for our employees?
- What is your dream for what we can do?
- What do you envision us being capable of achieving?
- What do you see as our strengths and capabilities?
- How is our company unique?

Clarifying Roles and Responsibilities

Clarity from upper management about roles and responsibilities can be quite valuable, especially in a rapidly changing work environment. Many are asked to do more with less, and people move in and out of positions and the company. People change, and organizations change; sometimes individual roles and responsibilities must be reshaped, shifted, or re-created. It's wise to check in about role clarity.

- What do you see as my role here?
- What is your role, and how can I support you in it?
- What do you expect of me? What do you want from me? What do you need from me?
- What do you see as my responsibilities?
- How can we work together?
- What am I accountable for?
- What are you responsible for, and how does my work support you?
- What do you see as the roles of the people I manage?
- Who else is invested in and affected by what we do?
- What are we creating?

Seeking Feedback

If your organization conducts performance reviews, you will almost certainly be getting a review of your work from time to time. Informal meetings with your leaders can also present good opportunities for seeking feedback. Taking time to request specific feedback shows your leaders that you are invested in learning and growing and that you can take criticism well. It demonstrates your engagement with the organization and how you fit into it.

- What words of wisdom can you give me?
- What would you do in my situation?
- What am I not considering? What have I not thought of yet?
- What opportunities do you see for me? What challenges do you see for me?
- What could I be doing better? Where can I grow?
- What do I need to keep doing, or do more of?
- What do I need to change?
- What do you think of how I handled [situation or task]?
- What do you wish I would do? What do you wish I would not do?
- How am I doing so far in this role? How could I do better?

What to Say When Things Go Wrong

When things go wrong—from a small glitch to a major catastrophe—you often need to seek guidance from your organization's leadership. You may be using the techniques covered in Chapter 10, Coaching Employee Performance after a Crisis, with your team. You can use some of those same phrases with your bosses, with a shift in focus. When asking the same questions of those above you, you will invite a bigger perspective that may help you recover from a problem or prevent the next one. You may have to acknowledge responsibility or explain your actions and those of your employees in some cases.

- I understand that you may be frustrated and angry about this situation.

- I accept responsibility for . . . .

- Here is what's happening. What are your thoughts?

- Here is what has already happened, and what we did (or will do) about it . . . .

- What are the larger effects of this problem?

- How do you want us to handle it? (How do you wish we had handled it?)

- How will you support us with creating the solution we want?

After a crisis has passed, checking in with managers above you can offer a higher level of perspective on the issues.

- From your perspective, where were the breakdowns?

- Was this problem something that could have been anticipated? What signs did we miss?

- Is this something that could happen again? How should we plan to prevent it?

- What did we learn from this issue?
- What needs to change because of this crisis?
- What positive lessons came out of this? [also share the lessons you and your employees learned]
- How well did we deal with this problem, in your opinion?
- What went right in this situation? What strengths were revealed?
- Who else needs to be informed of this situation and what we've learned?

Chapter 19
Relationship Building

B uilding a strong working relationship with those above you in the organization's hierarchy is smart. Relationships between all workers, no matter what their level, help groups come together to create amazing results. Whether it's a defined team or a lateral partnership, building strong relationships within an organization reaps positive benefits for all stakeholders. Note that it doesn't have to be a *personal* relationship—you don't have to share deep, dark secrets or bare your soul to another person. A working relationship is obviously about getting things done. If you cultivate those relationships in your own work, you are setting yourself up for delivering value and demonstrating your worth.

Creating a Working Relationship

Do you know how to work really well with your boss? Bosses are human, after all, and come with preferences and pet peeves, like anyone does. If you are aware of the personality quirks, working style, and values of your leaders, you can develop better relationships with them. Before talking to your boss, periodically ask yourself the following questions.

- What do I know and what have I noticed about my boss?
- How does he or she like to communicate with me?
- What is she responsible for? How does my work support that?
- How much supervision does he offer me? How much do I want?
- What's the most effective way for me to get what I want or need from my boss?
- What bothers my leaders? What are their pet peeves?
- How do they respond to and celebrate good news?
- How does my boss respond to problems and challenges?
- What have my leaders requested of me? How have they supported me?
- How does what I do support my leaders?

When you have the opportunity, you can speak directly with those above you about how they want to work with you. This might be especially wise when you have stepped into a new position or when there has been a change in the leadership of an organization. Building a strong, effective working relationship improves your own performance and likely that of your boss as well.

- How do you want me to keep you informed of what's going on?
- How frequently do you want contact with me?
- How much do you want to know about the details of what we are doing?
- What's a good way to approach you if something is going wrong?
- How much pushback do you want if we don't agree?
- What kinds of problems or issues do you want me to bring to your attention? What kinds of things do you want me to handle myself?
- How do you like to offer feedback? How do you want me to give you feedback?
- If I have a great idea to share, how should I convey it to you?
- How do you like to celebrate accomplishments and achievements?
- How do you like to work?
- What boundaries do you need me (and others) to respect?
- What do I need to know that will help me work with you even better?

Supporting Your Leaders

Just as your employees support you, you will support those above you. Being mindful of and cognizant that what you offer your leaders will point you in the right direction for creating strong relationships with them. Getting clear direction from them keeps everyone's performance pointed in the right direction.

- What are you responsible for, and how can I (and my team or department) support you?

- How can I make your job easier?

- What can I handle for you? What can I take off your plate that would make things easier?

- What can we create together?

- What are you looking for from me?

- How can we work and grow together in this area?

- How do our strengths, capabilities, and skills complement each other?

- I have an idea about something new we could do, and here's how it would support our work . . . .

- What if we did [task, procedure] differently? How might that improve our performance?

- How does our work support the mission of this organization? How could we do that even better?

- Here are some issues and challenges I want to tell you about . . . . How can we create solutions?

Acknowledging Your Leaders

I've said it several times before: We all like a pat on the back now and then. Those above you crave this acknowledgment just as much as a frontline employee does. Being a leader sometimes means making unpopular decisions and hearing complaints. Taking the time to acknowledge the positive, appreciating your boss, or just admitting that a job is difficult can go a long way toward building a strong relationship.

- I really appreciate your guidance on [specific task or issue].
- I learned a lot from you about . . . .
- Thank you for your support, it helped us all do better [give specific examples].
- I know it must not have been easy to [do a difficult task or make a decision, such as letting someone go].
- Here is what I noticed after you implemented that change or decision . . . .
- My staff are saying [good things] about you and your work with us.
- Thanks for clarifying [issue, problem, question] for me, I felt much more confident moving forward.
- I know that you work hard to get us the resources we need and advocate for us higher up in the organization. Thank you!
- It's been a difficult, chaotic time lately. Thanks for hanging in there with us!

Chapter 20

Change Initiatives and Working with Upper Leadership

F rom time to time, an organization will initiate a change deliberately, rather than just reacting to problems and issues. Sometimes these are very large changes that have significantly impacted how the organization does business. Major changes require vision, buy-in, and hard work. This chapter discusses how to work with your upper leadership during a big change. Chances are good that the leaders have decided to create this change and will rely on you to communicate it to the employees and help make it happen. This is covered in Chapter 8, Change Initiatives and Working with Employees. By talking with them about the ideas and concepts behind the change, you can find the key ideas and goals that will help motivate your employees to commit and then perform well.

Determining Purpose and Vision

A good change initiative is made with a specific purpose and vision in mind. This purpose should be communicated to all involved for several reasons. First, it will prove that the change has some thought behind it and isn't just another "flavor of the month" or some new fad. Second, it will allow employees to be invested in the outcome, engaged in the process, and committed to the change. Take some time with your immediate manager and other leaders above you to get a clear picture of the purpose and vision of the change initiative. Then you can take this vision back to your employees with the phrases offered in Chapter 8, Change Initatives and Working with Employees.

- What is the purpose of making this change? [listen for specifics and a vision]

- Once this change is in place, what will we be able to do?

- How does this change help us work toward our mission?

- What benefits will we see from this change?

- What are your thoughts about this change? I would like your opinion.

- How do you think it will affect us?

- What opportunities does this change open for you? For me? For our employees?

- What do you hope will happen as this change rolls out?

- How does this change help our organization grow?

- Where do you see problems or concerns related to this being accepted by the employees?

- What are your concerns moving forward? Who or what are you concerned about the most?

- How do we present this change to our employees to get the most buy-in?
- How do you want me to deal with resisters?
- What advice do you have for me and the rest of the employees before rolling this out?

Defining the Change Process

The process of a change initiative can be highly influenced by an organization's leaders. To keep things moving smoothly and everyone performing optimally, guidance from those above you can be incredibly helpful.

- Specifically, how will this change affect how we work? How will it change what we produce?
- What will our new procedures be?
- What will we no longer be doing?
- What will we be doing that's new?
- How are we supported in creating this change?
- How will you help us during the process of change?
- What resources are available to us as we make the change?
- What can we do to get ready?
- What advice would you give me to ensure this transition goes as smoothly as possible?

At various times in the change initiative, you will almost certainly be checking in with your leaders about how things are going. In addition to feeding back information to them, you can use the opportunity to get their opinions and thoughts.

- How are we doing? Are we on track for this change? Are we ready?
- What's next in the change process? Are we prepared for it?
- What is going well? What is not going so well?
- What else do we need to do to be prepared?
- How can we make it even better?
- How are we addressing resistance? Is it working?
- What else do we need to do or try?

Moving Forward

When a change initiative is complete, you will find a chance to review the process for key learnings and look ahead for new opportunities. Conferring with your managers, bosses, and leaders connects all levels of the organization in moving forward. It's also a great chance to acknowledge the hard work and leadership of everyone involved (see the section, Acknowledging Your Leaders, in Chapter 19). This will lay the groundwork for proactive and engaged performance for everyone.

- How well did we follow the plan for the change?
- Did we meet our goals and milestones? If so, how well did we do? If not, what got in our way?
- What are the results of the change? How do they measure up against what we hoped for?
- What were the surprises along the way? How do they affect us?
- Who stood out as rising to the challenge? Who were our advocates?
- What did we learn from our resisters?
- What strengths and capabilities were revealed during this change initiative?
- What were some of the unintended consequences, good and bad? How are we dealing with them?
- Now that we have completed this change, what opportunities and challenges lie ahead for this organization?
- What do we need to have in place or be aware of when another change initiative begins?
- How is our entire organization shaped by this change?

- How has creating this change helped us work toward our mission?
- How does this change affect our clients or customers?

About the Author

Laura Poole is an Associate Certified Coach (ACC), credentialed by the International Coach Federation. She is the founder of her own coaching practice, Archer Coaching, and specializes in helping working professionals create a meaningful career balanced with a joyful life. She works with teams, companies, and individuals to create lasting change, powerful results, and new ways of thinking and doing. She is also an avid public speaker on a variety of topics.

After graduating from Duke University, Laura began her career in publishing. She eventually founded her own freelance editorial services company in 1997, through which she provides scholarly copy editing for major publishers. She also codeveloped a respected editing training program for freelancers and publishers. Her shift into the coaching field came in 2007 when she decided to seek work that had a meaningful impact on the world. Visit her Web site at www.archercoaching.com.

Laura lives in Durham, North Carolina, with her family. You can reach her at laura@archercoaching.com.